N

Never Walk Alone

Gavin Peacock and Alan Comfort
with Alan MacDonald

HODDER AND STOUGHTON
LONDON SYDNEY AUCKLAND

British Library Cataloguing in Publication Data

A catalogue record for this book is available from
The British Library

ISBN 0 340 60675 4

Typeset by Hewer Text Composition Services, Edinburgh
Printed and bound in Great Britain by
Cox & Wyman Ltd, Reading, Berks.

Hodder and Stoughton Ltd
A division of Hodder Headline PLC
338 Euston Road
London NW1 3BH

Contents

Chapter One

Gallowgate

Gallowgate sits high on a hill above the city. It is a local name. The uninitiated ask for St James's Park, the home of Newcastle United. But on Saturdays Gallowgate is, as its name suggests, a place of public execution for visitors to the city.

By two o'clock on a Saturday large crowds have begun to gather for the spectacle. They wear the colours of their side: striped black-and-white shirts, black-and-white scarves, even zebra-painted faces that make them look like a distant Tyneside relative of the Maoris.

The noise steadily grows from a low drone to a buzz of anticipation and waves of chanting that spread across the terraces. At three o'clock the stadium erupts in a deafening roar heard all over the city as the two sides enter the arena. The colours of the other side make no difference – red, blue, white – they are only lambs for the slaughter. All eyes are on the eleven men in magpie black and white. A hush of expectancy falls before the start. Twenty-two players stand tensed, ready to strain every muscle and shed every drop of energy they possess. One man, all in black, raises an arm. The whistle goes. 30,000 voices urge on their side. Ninety minutes to settle the argument.

Gallowgate expects.

Of course we are only talking about a game of football. But try telling that to a Newcastle supporter. Or, for that matter, a Liverpool, Manchester United or Sunderland supporter. Tell it to Bill Shankly, Anfield's most celebrated manager who once famously remarked, 'Football's not a matter of life and death; it is more important than that.'

For the die-hard fan, Saturday is what makes the rest of the week worth living. Some matches can be boring or frustrating but there is always the expectation that a game will explode into life. At its best there are moments of raw emotion and excitement. When the ball bulges in the net, 30,000 fists punch the air in salute. Every one of them feels as if they are the one who has just scored. It is said in Newcastle that the pubs are like a morgue on Saturday night if United have lost. Football is more than a game. To its fans it is a religion followed by millions every week.

What is it like to be a professional footballer, to carry the hopes and dreams of thousands on your shoulders on a Saturday? Gavin Peacock and Alan Comfort have both played in front of the fanatical Gallowgate crowd. One as captain of the celebrated Newcastle side which won the first division in 1993, the other playing for local rivals, Middlesbrough.

They both have vivid memories of playing at St James's Park but for very different reasons. For Gavin Peacock, it is the ground where his name as a top-class footballer was made. He had played for other clubs – Queen's Park Rangers, Gillingham and Bournemouth – but it was at Newcastle that he began to attract the attention of the national press as well as the biggest names in the Premiership. In 1992 the legendary Kevin Keegan had just arrived as United's manager and the Magpies began the season with eleven straight wins. The famine of success on Tyneside had ended and the Geordie faithful came in their thousands each week to see their team return to the Premiership. None was a bigger favourite than Peacock; not only did Keegan make him captain for his inspirational performances, but he was idolised as a proven goalscorer. In the promotion year he spearheaded Newcastle's attack, netting eighteen times before injury prevented him adding to the tally. The previous season Peacock had scored twenty-one goals and been unanimously acclaimed Newcastle's Player of the Year. After three seasons the Gallowgate faithful knew they could rely on their captain to give everything in United's cause. On a Saturday it would take Gavin Peacock ten to fifteen minutes just to make his way through the packed crowds of autograph hunters from his car to the dressing-room.

'They're just totally fanatical and enthusiastic,' he says of the United supporters. 'People came up to me early in the promotion season and said, "You just don't know what it means to us to be up the top." It's a different world. 30,000 every week there. It was a total football environment. You lived football off the field as well as on it. My Newcastle experience is something I'll always treasure because I had a great relationship with the fans up there. I look back on it as a great three years.'

Alan Comfort's memories of playing at St James's Park are in stark contrast. It is where his nightmare began – the moment that every footballer dreads, when you feel something in your leg lock and you can't move it.

As a Middlesbrough player that day, 3 November 1989, Comfort was not expecting to receive much sympathy. As far as Newcastle supporters were concerned, Boro were held in only slightly less contempt than the poisonous Mackems (Sunderland).

'As soon as you come out you receive hate from the terraces because you're not their team,' remembers Comfort. 'Wherever you get a really passionate crowd like the Newcastle one, that same kind of feeling that lifts a team is also against the other team. You sense that and it's very intimidating when you come out. It's actually quite a violent atmosphere to come into. The stadium is balanced precariously on a knife edge ready to spill over into physical violence itself. The tension transmitted from the terraces just grips you and it suddenly feels as if you have lost control. This isn't just a game of football, it's actually much more than that.

'At moments like that, I think many footballers are motivated by fear, a kind of survival instinct bred by the overwhelming pressure from the terraces. Even the Newcastle players must be gripped by the same fear because if the unthinkable happens and the game goes wrong, the hatred will be turned on them instead.'

Comfort had only arrived at Middlesbrough that season. It was his eighteenth game for the club and he was playing at the peak of his career. But where Gallowgate was the springboard for Gavin Peacock's rise to football stardom, it was to prove the burial ground for Alan Comfort's dreams. In the second half he left the field on a stretcher. As he was carried off, questions surfaced in his mind through the pain: what was wrong with his knee? How bad was the injury? How long before he'd be back? Nothing could have prepared him to find out that he was leaving the professional game never to return again.

At the age of only twenty-four, he had apparently passed in the space of a few seconds from being a rising star to landing on life's scrapheap. What sort of future was there for him without football? How was he to come to terms with never playing again? How was he going to support his family? These were the questions that began to haunt him in the following year as he went from one surgeon to the next.

At the end of that year, by a cruel twist of irony, Gavin Peacock arrived in the north-east to play for Newcastle.

The two players had known each other since they were teenagers at Queen's Park Rangers and had become close friends. Now, at the very point Comfort's career was in tatters, Peacock's rise to the top was just about to achieve lift off.

Neither of them fits the stereotype of a footballer who 'just wants to do the business on Saturday, Brian'. Gavin Peacock is self-assured and quietly articulate, the product of a famous footballing father. Alan Comfort by contrast is energetic and talkative, the kind of person who would find it hard to wait long on a street corner without something extraordinary happening to him.

In a way, the pair represent the two faces of football – success and heartbreak, triumph and disaster. At the beginning of every match a coin is spun. As it turns in the air it symbolises the element of luck that is a part of every sport. 'It wasn't our day, we just had no luck,' moans the manager whose team has just lost. Many people would describe what happened to Alan Comfort in the same vein – just another case of cruel luck. While Peacock's life has been successful, Comfort's has apparently been a sad waste. But there may be another way of looking at what happened. To understand it you have to hear their stories for yourself.

Chapter Two

The Quiet Boy who Played Football

'The best fourteen-year-old player I've ever seen.' That was the verdict of Queen's Park Rangers' manager, Tommy Docherty, on Alan Comfort. Docherty, a flamboyant Scot who once boasted, 'I've had more clubs than Jack Nicklaus,' had seen more players than most. His career in management took in Chelsea, Rotherham, QPR (twice), Aston Villa, Porto, Hull (assistant manager), Scotland, Manchester United, Derby, Sydney Olympic and Wolves. During his roller-coaster ride through football, thousands of young hopefuls must have passed before his eyes, each dreaming he might be the next Charlton or Best. Alan Comfort must have had prodigious ability at fourteen for Docherty to single him out.

Comfort himself heard the comment via QPR's chief scout, Chris Geeler. What sort of ideas does that kind of praise put in the mind of an impressionable fourteen year old? The teenager must have felt little doubt he would make it as a professional footballer. He must have dreamed of stardom, multi-million pound transfers and pulling on the number eleven shirt for England. At fourteen it all lay before Alan Comfort. The world was at his feet – at least, the football world and that was the only one that mattered. The thought that he might fail would hardly have entered his head.

Alan Comfort was born in Aldershot just before the Christmas of 1964. As the fourth arrival in the Comfort family he was destined to feel outnumbered and, in some ways, overshadowed by his three elder sisters.

'My mother always says that my dad would have kept going until he got a boy, so she was just relieved to see me,' says Comfort.

All the family lived in the Aldershot area. Alan's grandfather on his mother's side was evacuated along with thousands of other children during the war and placed in foster care when peace came. He never knew who or where his parents were, so the Comfort family tree doesn't go back far on one side. Alan's father, George Comfort, worked in the newspaper print business producing local papers such as *The Aldershot News*. These days the print jobs have long gone, but for Comfort senior it provided a steady job if not a highly paid one. At weekends he would play football, both Saturday and Sunday, for local amateur sides. Football was the passion of his life and he was anxious that his son should share it.

'You never knew much about his job or his money, he keeps things close to his chest,' says Alan. 'But a lot of the people that he worked with played football. I remember going to the football with them and that would have been from a very young age. I think I played one of my first games of football when I was about four years old, so my dad must have been playing football with me before that. I played for an under-sevens team, and that was the beginning. I must have been so small – it's incredible to think of it – but I can remember playing those games. I don't remember much about my childhood except football – that dominates a lot of it.'

George Comfort was not a man to talk much about his feelings, but his pride in his son's football career is there for anyone to see. With four children to feed there was never much money to spare in the Comfort household, but what there was would always be put aside to buy young Alan's boots and football kit. No doubt there were times his three elder sisters felt they were the victims of unjust favouritism. Their father would drive his son anywhere to see him play football. Today he has a collection of five scrapbooks filled with programmes and press-cuttings that record every major event in Alan's career, from youth games to the final season with Middlesbrough. They say more than any words what Alan's success meant to his father.

Parental pride can easily become pressure, but Alan denies being pushed into football. What pressure existed was of an unspoken kind because from an early age it was clear where he was heading.

'They never said to me, "You're never going to be able to do this, you've got to buckle down, you can do better." My dad would never have done that. He always let me get on with it. But when I played badly I knew he was disappointed just from his face and some of the comments he would make. It meant something to him. He couldn't have travelled all those times when I was a kid, spending all his money that he didn't really have, and not felt disappointment. I knew there was a pressure to succeed. It came from my family and it came from outside.'

There is a telling story when Alan was fifteen. From the top of the stairs he overheard a conversation between his parents that was about him. They were discussing whether he really was good enough to make it as a professional footballer. Alan recalls that he was devastated. He knew he was *meant* to be a footballer; his whole life was planned towards that goal. If his parents weren't sure, where did that leave him?

There was little reason to doubt. As a young schoolboy Alan's ability was so obvious that he was playing for the

Aldershot and Farnborough District side alongside boys
two or three years his senior. From there he progressed
to the under-thirteen side where football began to be a
serious business. The manager was Charlie Mortimer,
a former Chelsea and England amateur who had dedicated his life to coaching schools' football. Mortimer put
together a side from the cream of Surrey and Hampshire
schoolboys. There were eleven county players with Comfort as captain. Nearly every one of them later joined
professional clubs but, such are the odds against success,
that only three eventually made the grade. Alan Comfort
was the first.

For his twelfth birthday treat, Alan accompanied his
dad to Stamford Bridge to watch Chelsea play. The game
was against Wolves in the top of the table, second-division
clash. Chelsea, under Eddie McCreadie, were making a
comeback as one of the glamour clubs of London, and
were about to return to the top flight.

'It was the most incredible experience,' says Alan looking back. 'I was totally overawed by it all. I remember
coming out. It was so packed in the ground that all the
kids were on their fathers' shoulders.'

Only a year later, George Comfort was in the shower
when he received a phone call. It was Chelsea football
club asking if his son Alan would be interested in coming
to train at the ground.

Would he be *interested*? It was the telephone call every
schoolboy dreamed of. Alan recalls that he was both
excited and scared by the prospect. 'It was an amazing
feeling to think that suddenly you were going to go in
and play for a professional club, but also quite frightening
because there are loads of kids. Our first training sessions
built up to a trial game. That's the way they do it. And you
wonder how you're going to do, because all the kids want
to do well. Throughout my career I was always fortunate
to be able to produce my best in the first game when you're

so keen to make a lasting impression. I remember scoring lots of goals in that first game and then clicking straight into the fact that I was going to be a player they would work with. I knew that from the start.'

Comfort might have gone on to play for Chelsea, the club Gavin Peacock plays for today, but for the fact that football clubs do not recognise the law of 'we saw him first'. By his fourteenth birthday, Comfort had received approaches from enough football clubs to make even Tommy Docherty jealous. It became almost commonplace for the phone to ring with an enquiry from a scout at Fulham, QPR or Manchester United. He played in a trial game at Crystal Palace and scored five goals – not surprisingly they urged him to sign on the dotted line there and then.

In the end the choice came down to the London clubs as the teenager couldn't imagine living away from home. He was training at QPR when the comment was passed on from Tommy Docherty. The glowing praise may have been intended to influence but QPR had other less subtle means of persuasion. Football clubs are not above using any legal means to get a talented young player to sign against fierce competition. While most fourteen year olds were playing over the park and saving money from their paper round, Alan Comfort was staying in five-star hotels for the summer holiday to be near the training ground. The bill was footed by QPR.

'They used to say to me things like, "Have you got a friend you want to bring with you?" So I'd bring a mate up from school and he would come and be part of it all, just so that I had some company. It was amazing the kind of things that went on.

'My parents would come up with me to the hotel and we didn't know quite what to do because you had all these things. It's nice to have steak and chips one night if you never normally have it, but when you can have it every night and every lunchtime, you don't really know what's happening to you. Then you go out and they would buy you the best football gear and the best clothes. If you wanted a bicycle, they bought you the best racing bike that you could get (the only bikes I ever had, my grandad used to make for me when I was growing up). I remember the pride I felt riding to school on that bicycle. They also bought me a big hi-fi set.'

Not every teenager would have been courted with this sort of incentive. Rangers knew they were facing tough competition from glamour clubs like Manchester United, and they could see in Comfort a potential star of the future. Other players had graduated through their youth policy, names such as Clive Allen and Paul Goddard. At that age if a young star slips through the net a club may end up paying a million pounds for him later on. What is the cost of a racing bike and a hi-fi in comparison?

At fourteen there is no compulsion for a schoolboy to sign a contract tying him to one club. Gavin Peacock waited until he had reached the relatively mature age of seventeen. The difference was that he could draw on the advice of a father who was a former footballer and a manager himself. George Comfort was more used to printing headlines than negotiating contracts with the football clubs who made them. It was left to Alan to make up his own mind.

'For somebody like me, it was important to go to one place and to build a career,' says Alan with hindsight. 'It was awkward having so many options. In a way you just wanted to get on with playing football. So I decided that as a fourteen year old I would sign for Queen's Park Rangers.

'After I signed I found out that other good players had signed for lots of money, because even schoolboys get money to sign. But you have to ask for it, to fight for it. It never entered my parents' minds, nor mine. There are no regrets really, but my dad sometimes looks back on it and wonders if he should have handled things differently.'

One clause that was written into the contract guaranteed Comfort an apprenticeship at the age of sixteen. With most young players the club will wait to make a decision at that stage, but Rangers evidently wanted to protect their investment.

Comfort left school with six 'O' levels to start his apprenticeship. Although it was a solid achievement, education had taken a back seat from the moment professional football had beckoned. The school turned a blind eye to the days he skipped classes to go training.

Doubtless many of Comfort's school friends would have given anything to trade places with him. They might be surprised today to hear him argue that football demanded a high price for its rewards.

'In the early years the price that I paid was that I was always playing all the time. But you don't mind that when you're a kid – it's fun, and you play four or five games a week.

'Then you hit a certain age when your friends are not playing football anymore every night of the week because they have found other things – girlfriends, discos or going to the pubs. When you get to that age you find that your friends are all experimenting with everything life has to offer.

'Looking back on it, it's not as if I would have been able to do it any differently, but I did miss out on part of growing up, on some of those friendships that I would have had. I worked in a world that meant I travelled an hour and then just played football. Everything was very serious and it meant money. It meant money to me but it was also big business to everybody else, so it was important that you weren't out the night before a game. There were so many games it was bound to affect your social life.'

It was not just among his friends that Alan felt different.

In his family he was quickly labelled by relatives as the 'quiet boy who plays football'. It was a tag he was to tire of in later life.

'I always laugh about this but we've got a big family and in family gatherings they're only now beginning to try and adapt to not asking me something about football when they first see me. When I finished playing football I did some commentary for a radio station. Everybody in the family just diverted to saying, "How's the football going on the radio?" In fact I was only doing that once every couple of weeks and the rest of my life was still going on, yet they couldn't get out of football mode. I was associated with football and people couldn't communicate to me as a person if it wasn't about football.

'Looking back I don't want to say that I didn't enjoy it, because I did. I enjoyed being a star wherever I went. Whenever I turned up at a football match I knew that the other team had seen me come and were thinking, "Oh no, he's playing." All of my mates from school were so pleased I was going to be there because they knew they would win now. There is that sense of importance, but it's all wrapped up in football. What I would say is that all that was wonderful as a kid was part of what was difficult to deal with when I got to eighteen or nineteen and nobody said, "Wonderful," anymore.'

It is the classic story of the child prodigy. The sport and entertainment worlds are full of cases where precocious talent has been hard to live up to later on. What happened to Buster Mottram, Justin Fashanu and countless others? For Alan Comfort success came easily until the age of eighteen and then it had to be worked for.

As a sixteen-year-old apprentice at Queen's Park Rangers, he was still on an upward curve. The management team at QPR was one which could hardly have been more impressive. While the charismatic Terry Venables ran the first team, the ex-Arsenal duo Frank McClintock and George Graham looked after the reserves and youth team respectively.

Graham has gone on to be one of the most successful managers in the game at Arsenal. Comfort describes his apprenticeship under him as 'probably the best any player could have'. Graham had been a cultured midfielder and a key player in Arsenal's double winning side of 1971. He expected a lot from the young players he coached, but then he never asked them to do something he couldn't do himself.

'In football you earn respect,' says Comfort. 'That's why most managers have been there and played. On free kicks and set plays George Graham would ask us to do incredible things. We did all the things that Arsenal still do now. He would set them up and then finish them himself. A volley from twenty yards and he would put it in the top corner. There was tremendous respect from us as sixteen year olds. He worked on discipline – that was the key. We worked hard as a team. We didn't have the best team but we won everything. That seems to me to be the secret of his success. It was important as a kid to learn the discipline of what was expected of you.'

With Graham at the helm, QPR's youth team swept to success winning the South East Counties League. Success meant attention, and one man to take notice was the England youth manager, at that time John Cartwright (later to be succeeded by a manager called Graham Taylor). On 11 March 1982 a letter arrived for Alan Comfort from Lancaster Gate. It informed him that he had been selected as one of five QPR players for the England Youth Squad to play in an international tournament in the south of France. It was Comfort's first England call-up, and a moment to savour.

'I remember driving home from the training ground. I was driving so fast and feeling so excited because it dawned on me that I was playing for England. As I saw it at that moment in time, I was one of the best players in the country. Or even more frightening, I was the best player in my position in the country. That's quite an amazing feeling.

'I suppose I was a bit big-headed because I was on a roller-coaster. I was on my way somewhere and no one else was coming with me. At that point you think that you deserve it, that you're actually good enough for it. You think, "I'm right for this." You're not overawed at all. "I'm playing for my country but I'm good enough. I'm not going to let anybody down."'

Comfort didn't let anyone down on that trip. The England team reached the final, beating Poland and the favourites, Holland, on the way. In the final they were to meet France, and Comfort found himself closely marked in the game. Michel Hidalgo of the French national team had already singled him out as a star of the future.

'The English made the best impression,' he said in a French newspaper. 'I was particularly impressed by the number nine, Alan Comfort of Queen's Park Rangers. One must find him with the élite soon.'

Surprisingly England lost the final 1–0, but Comfort's all-round performance in the tournament was good enough to ensure he was picked for the next tour three months later. This time the host country was Norway, with Poland and Denmark also taking part. England started the tournament as favourites but for QPR's young winger the tour was to end in disgrace. Things got off on a bad foot with the first game against Norway when England were trounced 4–0. It had not gone according to the script and the players trooped off at the final whistle looking shell shocked.

The next game was against Denmark two days later. The England squad trained on the Wednesday evening and were then given time off to prepare for the important second game the next day. In Norway it remained light throughout the summer nights so few of the players felt inclined to retire to their rooms. Comfort recalls how he decided on a walk into the town of Levanger with two other players – Paul Rideout (then with Swindon) and Paul Brown of Aston Villa. It was a decision all three were to regret. Comfort tells the story today with a wry grin but at seventeen the incident could have sent his career into freefall.

'We went out after training just for a walk. We walked down into the town, met some people and went back to two girls' houses. Nothing happened; it wasn't anything incredible. They were quite near to the complex where we were staying. All we did was chat, but we lost our awareness of time because it was broad daylight. Suddenly we thought we had better go back because we had to be in by ten and we hadn't gone out till eight. We realised it was after ten and we panicked. Our panic was such that we made one bad decision. We hadn't done anything wrong, we were only a little bit late. Because we panicked we thought that the best thing we could do was wait until it quietened down and then sneak in. So we waited and waited until we thought that nobody was around. We weren't meant to be out, we knew we were in the wrong, nobody was denying that. So we sneaked into the hotel and just as we got a hand on the door the manager came out. "You stupid, stupid boys," he said, and told us he'd see us in the morning.

'We were desperate, we didn't know what to do. It was all so immature. You're seventeen years old, you're just a bit late and instead of walking through the gates and saying, "I'm really sorry. We've made a bad mistake here", we just panicked and did the wrong things. In the morning the manager called a team meeting and said, "I'm sending three players home on the first plane." That was it. Devastation.'

The punishment may seem harsh but all-England tours

operate on a strict code of discipline. The night before
an important international was not the time to bend
the rules. Worse still, no one was likely to believe the
players' version of events. When three teenagers roll back
well after midnight the obvious explanations are drink,
women or both. Comfort still protests to this day that
nothing happened. A claim that is made more believable
because it makes the whole episode laughable rather than
scandalous.

'Nobody ever believed us,' he smiles ruefully. 'I want
to be able to say we had a night of passion and it was all
worthwhile, but looking back on it we were sent home
for something that was just a waste of time. We got it
all wrong but we were young and when you're young you
make mistakes. On the flight back home I remember Paul
Rideout saying, "I hope the plane crashes." I seriously
think he meant it. We knew that when we got to the
other end our clubs would be waiting for us. It was a
huge embarrassment to them.'

To make matters worse the England youth side were
left with only ten fit players for the game the next day. Ian
Andrews, a goalkeeper, was drafted in to take Comfort's
place on the left wing. Naturally he turned in a good
performance as the team beat Denmark.

Back at London Airport, a grim-faced reception com-
mittee waited at the gate to meet the players. It included
representatives from the FA and QPR, Swindon and
Aston Villa. George Graham was absent, keeping himself
aloof from the low farce, but Alan's dad was there, along
with a few members of the press who scented the faint whiff
of scandal. It wasn't a story that hit national headlines but
a local paper ran a piece branding Alan Comfort as the
bad boy of Shepherd's Bush. It was the young apprentice's
first lesson in dealing with the press. The reporter who
interviewed him seemed genuinely sympathetic and then
wrote an article which slated him in the harshest terms.

It is one cutting that doesn't appear in George Comfort's scrapbooks.

QPR suspended him for two weeks and fined him £45. It could have been worse. What worried Comfort more was the effect the episode would have on his career. Would he ever play for England again? More urgently, with his eighteenth birthday approaching, would QPR offer him a professional contract? The question hung over him like a cloud between July and December. The club had advised him to get his head down and work hard but there was a heavy hint that he had damaged his chances.

8 December 1982 arrived. Alan Comfort's eighteenth birthday. No one at Queen's Park Rangers mentioned a contract to him. Eventually word came that he was to go and see Terry Venables after training. He went and sat outside the manager's office. The clock ticked by half an hour, an hour, two hours, three. In the office the voices of George Graham and Terry Venables could be heard in deep discussion. Comfort shifted restlessly in his seat. 'It must be a close call,' he thought. 'I wonder who's arguing for me and who's against me? Do they think I'm good enough or not?'

Finally he was called in. Venables smiled, shook his hand and offered him a three-year contract.

Comfort has never found out how much he figured in what Venables and Graham were discussing. It is likely that there were other things on their mind besides the contract of one apprentice. But Comfort believes they kept him waiting to make a point.

'In a way I think I deserved it because of what I'd done. I'd embarrassed the club. I think it was their way of saying, "We're in charge of this; it's an important decision. You cannot just walk into things and out of things. Everything is not in your control; we control your future." I learnt a lesson really. It wasn't all easy. Everything had worked until then; there was never any doubt I'd be an apprentice.

Then suddenly there was a doubt. I didn't know whether or not they would keep me. Then you don't know what you're going to do.'

The 'bad boy' tag was to stay with him for some years as a joke that other players would bring up from time to time. Comfort never did play another international for England but it wasn't because the FA never forgave him. Within a year he was playing in friendlies at Aston Villa and Stoke for England youth sides. Graham Taylor (then manager of Watford) was building his side for the European Championships and Comfort, in the end, did not figure in his plans.

The immediate future was as a professional with Queen's Park Rangers, trying to get into the first team. With the astute Venables in charge it was a golden age in QPR's history, recalling the days when Rodney Marsh helped them win the League Cup. In 1982–3, the season Comfort turned professional, QPR were second-division champions, ten points clear of their nearest rivals, Wolves. They went on the following season to finish fifth in the first division and reach the final of the FA Cup. For a player just starting his professional career, Rangers should have been the dream club, but often in football it works the other way around. A successful side is a settled side. In the 1983–4 season Venables kept faith with a squad of around fourteen players. There was no room for the promising left-winger from Aldershot.

'The rest of us could have scored ten goals in the reserves and we still wouldn't have got in,' reflects Comfort. 'As a kid that was the point where you hit a stop. There was no way your career could move on because you're in the middle of a bottleneck. It needed to move to allow players to progress, but the problem was that part of the club was doing so well that everything else got held up.'

If things were settled on the field, they soon received a shake-up in the management side. In May 1984 Venables left for the lure of Spain and Barcelona. George Graham also left, to the less glamorous prospect of managing Millwall. The names who had signed Alan Comfort were gone and he was soon to feel his own time was running out at Queen's Park Rangers.

It led to two momentous decisions – one that Alan Comfort looks back on as the biggest mistake of his career, the other that he considers the most important decision of his life.

Chapter Three

Peacock and Son

Whatever the future holds, the name of Peacock is already guaranteed a place in the football hall of fame. Not for a record number of goals, appearances or international caps, but for one of those odd moments of history that sometimes sneak up and tap an unsuspecting person on the shoulder.

In the August of 1965, Keith Peacock, a young professional at Charlton Athletic, had been in and out of the first team and was desperately hoping that this would be the season when he would establish himself. Charlton's manager at the time was Bob Stokoe – a man who was later to have his own moment of destiny when he danced onto the Wembley turf in his lucky shoes after Sunderland had beaten Leeds United in the 1973 FA Cup final. On this Saturday though, Stokoe was more concerned with the less glamorous prospect of facing Bolton Wanderers on the opening day of the season. He took Peacock aside to break the bad news: the twenty year old was not to be in the line-up that day. Like any young player left out, Peacock was bitterly disappointed, but the blow was softened slightly by the news that he would be on the bench as substitute. Today few games go by without a sub. making an appearance because of injury or tactics, but in 1967 to be named as substitute was as novel as colour television.

Peacock needn't have worried. Within ten minutes of the kick off he was stripping off his tracksuit to go on. The Charlton goalkeeper had been injured and the side had to be reshuffled with another player going between the posts. It wasn't until that evening, on a train heading home from Manchester to London, that Keith Peacock realised he had made footballing history. There on the back of an evening paper was the headline: 'First substitute – Keith Peacock.'

Today Keith Peacock is in his late forties, although only the greying hair gives him away: his body still has the lean, muscular build of a footballer. His own father came from South Shields and was a useful enough footballer to have represented the town. Keith was born in London after his parents came south to look for work during the depression. Yet despite Arsenal, Chelsea and Tottenham being on his doorstep, it was his father's beloved Newcastle who first caught Keith's imagination. In those heady days it was 'Wor Jackie', the great Jackie Milburn who was the pride of United. The first cup final that captured ten-year-old Keith's imagination was in 1955 when Milburn scored the first goal to beat Manchester City. From that day on Keith was hooked on Newcastle United.

'When you have a team from that age it stays with you for ever because those are such impressionable years,' he explains. 'I was brought up as a Newcastle supporter and later on I watched them whenever they came to London. I'd get butterflies in my stomach just watching them play.'

Keith had to wait seventeen years to play at St James's Park himself. Something always seemed to prevent it until his final season in 1979. On that day Charlton lost 5–3 against a Newcastle team with the freescoring Peter Withe up front. Little did Keith Peacock know that thirteen years later his own son would pull on the black and white of the Magpies and captain the team which took Newcastle back to the Premiership.

Keith Peacock's playing career with Charlton lasted from 1962 to 1979 in which time he made over 500 appearances for the London club. It says something about the way football has changed in the eighties and nineties that Gavin has already played for five clubs at the age of twenty-five, still only half way through his career.

These days Gavin's father is back with Charlton again as reserve team manager. He first went into coaching in America, then followed management posts with Tampa Bay Rowdies, Gillingham, QPR and Maidstone United before returning to his old haunt at Charlton. For a brief period at Gillingham he belonged to that élite club of managers who have had their own sons playing for them. It is hardly surprising that as a former professional and a manager he has been the single greatest influence on his son's career.

Gavin was born in 1967 in Welling, south-east London. The family had put down roots in the area over many years. Gavin had grandparents, uncles, aunts and cousins all living close by, and much of his early life was taken up with family visits. Gavin has only fleeting memories of the house in Oakhampton Crescent, Welling. Typically for a footballer, he remembers more about the local park.

'A group of us local kids used to meet over there and play football,' he remembers. 'At one stage I tried to start my own football team up. We called it the Rainbow Team because when you are kids you've all got your favourite team's kit – Arsenal or West Ham or Tottenham. I thought there would be loads of different colours so we called it the Rainbow Team. I had the idea that we pay our subs every week and then after so many weeks we'd have enough to buy our kit for ourselves.'

Like most boyhood schemes, the Rainbows kept going for a few weeks and then faded away. But even in those early days, Gavin stood out among his friends as a natural leader.

When Gavin was eight the family moved to a large house ten minutes away in Barnshurst, Kent. It is still the house where Gavin visits his parents today and the rooms hold many childhood memories for him. From the lounge, french windows open out onto a wide garden, almost entirely laid to lawn. It wasn't that way when the family arrived, but Keith Peacock soon set about clearing the shrubs and levelling the ground. To an eight year old it must have seemed like having your own private five-a-side pitch in the back garden.

'This house seemed massive to us,' agrees Gavin. 'It's quite a decent-sized house anyway, but when we came it seemed huge. My sister and I would be out riding our bikes up and down all the time, and we used to be out in the garden a lot playing because we'd never had a garden that big before.'

Many professionals long to have a son follow in their footsteps. Was Gavin groomed for football from the day he could walk? Keith Peacock considers the question. 'There was never any pressure . . . but there was no shortage of encouragement,' he adds with a smile. Looking at an old cine film recently, he couldn't help noticing the six or seven footballs placed strategically around the garden so that wherever young Gavin went there was the chance to kick a ball.

At the age of seven, Gavin was presented with his first Newcastle kit. His father remembers the occasion well because it was a stern test of his resolve not to put any pressure on his son to play football.

'Looking back I suppose I was getting more of a thrill of seeing him in it than he was. He put his new kit on and I got ready for a session over the park. Then there was a knock at the door. It was a friend of his called Clinton. He said, "Hello Gavin. I've just come to see if you want to do some sewing with me. I've got some lovely new material." And Gavin said, "Oh yeah! Great! Bye then dad," and dropped the football.'

Keith Peacock bit his tongue on that occasion and he continued to keep himself in check when Gavin starting playing for teams. On Saturday mornings he would often go to watch his son play for school or district sides and then turn out for Charlton in the afternoon. He was a familiar local figure to the other parents on the touchline who must have wondered why someone who knew so much about football kept so quiet.

'You would hear parents on the sideline yelling and shouting at their kids and other kids and the referee and everyone,' says Keith. 'I would just stand and say nothing – not a word. People probably thought I'd lost my voice.'

It wasn't that he was indifferent to how Gavin played in a game. On the contrary, he admits that watching his son has always been one of his greatest pleasures in life. The silence was due to a conscious decision not to push or pressurise his son. Gavin remembers that he would usually get a quiet word of advice or praise after a game, but his father would never say anything in public.

If the young Gavin Peacock had shown no interest in football, or had shown no spark of natural ability, one wonders how easily his father would have accepted the fact. As it was, the problem didn't arise. Gavin was never short of talent or enthusiasm right from the start. It could have been a great handicap to have had a father who was a well-known professional footballer. Many sons or daughters with famous sporting parents have found their mother or father a hard act to follow. Yet Gavin Peacock's case is different. He would be the first to admit his debt to his father in helping his career. By taking a 'hands-off approach', his parents have been very careful not to saddle him with high expectations. The result is that Gavin has always felt free to draw on his father's experience and advice without living in his shadow. What difference might it have made to the wayward genius of a George Best or a Paul Gascoigne if they had had a father like Keith Peacock to turn to? Best himself complains, 'I have been saying for years that there is a need for someone to look after young professionals but I do not know one club that has ever done anything about it . . . I think that is why so many players get into trouble – they have no one to advise them; they have no one to turn to when things go wrong.'[1]

Gavin Peacock knows the truth of those words. In every decision of his career – from signing as a professional to agreeing million-pound transfer deals – his father has been at his shoulder to offer advice when asked.

During his junior school years, Gavin can remember going to Charlton Athletic to watch his father play. Surprisingly, he wasn't that interested. At that stage he was much keener to play football than watch it. Twice he was given the honour of leading Charlton out as team mascot at the Valley Ground. To run out with a professional side in front of thousands of home fans is a nerve-wracking experience for any young boy, but it is typical of Gavin's natural enthusiasm that he was keen to show what he could do.

'I was really keyed up for it because everyone in the dressing-room was geeing each other up before the game and I was really nervous standing there among all those professionals. Then I went out and I warmed the keeper up, had a few shots at him. I remember I wanted to do well, so I was trying to score past him all the time and knock them in the corners. Of course, when the mascot puts one in the crowd gives a cheer so I was getting very encouraged. The keeper wasn't very happy at all because he just wanted a feel of the ball – usually you're supposed to knock it into his hands. But I kept knocking it in the

net and he had to bend down, pick it up and give it to
me again.'

Life would have gone on happily enough in Kent for the
Peacock family but for the fact that a golden opportunity
presented itself in 1979. Keith Peacock finished his long
playing career that year at the age of thirty-five. He
now wanted to go into coaching. The first offer he
got was a six-month contract in America for a team in
Columbus, Ohio.

In the seventies soccer had taken off in America.
Although it was past the honeymoon period, when players
like Pelé and Rodney Marsh thrilled the crowds, it was still
big business.

Columbus Magic were in the American Soccer League,
a minor relative of the National League (NASL) which
boasted outlandish names like the Caribous of Colorado
and the Jacksonville Teamen as well as the mighty New
York Cosmos and Tampa Bay Rowdies. But Columbus
offered a first step in coaching for Keith Peacock and also
offered a free holiday in America for the family.

At the end of the summer eleven-year-old Gavin
returned home to start at Bexley Grammar School. But
then came a phone call from his father who had stayed out
in America to see Columbus Magic through the play-offs.
Keith Peacock had been approached by Gordon Jago,
the former Millwall manager then in charge of Tampa
Bay Rowdies. Jago remembered Keith Peacock from his
London days and knew that he was looking to go into
coaching. He wanted him to fly to Florida to discuss the
possibility of becoming assistant manager at Tampa.

It was a big decision because it meant a move to Florida
for two years and a step into the unknown. The Columbus
trip had been like a long holiday but this was a bigger
commitment. Gavin was only a month into secondary
school and both he and his sister would have to adjust
to school in America and leave behind all their family in

London. But it was too great an opportunity to miss. For the children, Gavin and Lauren, going to live in Florida USA, land of palm trees, golden beaches and Disneyworld – was a dream come true. Even today Gavin can transmit some of the wide-eyed wonder he felt as a child at the adventure.

'We thought it was great fun and very exciting, especially as my dad had a friend at the airport who got us into first class going over there. There was all this champagne going around, so we loved it. When we got there we were taken to a lovely hotel – Tampa Bay is set right in the Gulf of Mexico. We could have whatever we wanted.'

Of course, there was the subject of school to be settled. The Peacocks were very anxious that their children should get a good education since Gavin would be starting 'O' level courses on his return to England and Lauren entering secondary school. In the end, Tampa Bay paid for the two to attend a private school. Twelve-year-old Gavin found himself mixing with the sons and daughters of Florida's high society – lawyers, doctors and plastic surgeons. A limey in a school for rich American kids could easily have become a lonely outsider. It says a lot about young Gavin that he was quickly accepted. Maybe it was his wholehearted enthusiasm in everything coupled with his ability on the sports field and in class that won him friends.

The school was set in grounds fringed with palm trees and had every facility, including a beautiful library. Each day Lauren and Gavin would wait for the yellow school-bus to come and pick them up, just the way they had seen in countless American films. Gavin soon discovered that as a twelve-year-old footballer, he was a long way ahead of his classmates. He swiftly became the school soccer team's star player (which can't have done his popularity any harm). The effect on his football was instant.

'I was one of the top players all of a sudden. I'd been a

good player at home in England, but suddenly I was the top player and I could do what I wanted on the field. I could express myself. I used to try different things, maybe things I wouldn't have done at home, and as an individual I became better.'

Off the soccer field he joined the track team in athletics and worked hard in the classroom. But the best thing about school in Florida was that the summer holidays lasted three months. The Peacocks had the luxury of a private swimming pool and many long hot summer days were spent at the poolside. Weekends were dominated by football. Gavin played for a Sunday soccer team and on afternoons the whole family would go to watch Tampa Bay Rowdies. In 1980 the Rowdies boasted players like the flamboyant English striker, Frank Worthington, as well as a sprinkling of South American internationals.

Watching a major NASL soccer game is an experience far removed from standing on the terraces in England. Attending Tampa Bay's home games was a day out for the whole family with a party atmosphere. Stand in the car park outside the stadium a couple of hours before kick off and you would see families arriving to set up their barbeques and hand round Coke and hot dogs to the children. Inside the carnival atmosphere was stepped up with music, cheerleaders and all the razzmatazz that is part of the American sporting tradition. At that time the Rowdies could attract up to 65,000 fans to a top home game (bigger than any crowds at Anfield or Old Trafford) and the word hooliganism would not even have been whispered in the ground. As Keith Peacock puts it, 'In terms of selling the product it was quite phenomenal.'

The NASL wasn't short of ideas to market soccer differently. They introduced novelties such as sudden death extra time (next goal wins) and the 'Shootout' to replace penalties which weren't thought dramatic enough as a decider. For the Shootout, the shooter started from a thirty-five-yard line and had five seconds to score a goal against a keeper from the moment the linesman dropped his flag, à la motor racing. To English ears it may sound bizarre, and it was true that some American players were still grappling with the more traditional rules of soccer. An impressive list of European and South American players had to be imported to give the NASL star quality. As far as Gavin Peacock was concerned this was the real draw.

He got a job as a runner in the dressing-rooms. The duties were to help the kit manager or physio. with anything that needed doing. Gavin would help lay out the kit, run and fetch more ice and prepare the players' drinks. At the end of the game he might get a five- or ten-dollar tip from the coach or kit manager. But the money wasn't the biggest attraction. Gavin was assigned to the away-team dressing-rooms. There he met players who belong in the pantheon of world football greats: Franz Beckenbauer, the Brazilian Carlos Alberto, Johann Nieskins of Holland. For any young boy the chance to shake his heroes by the hand and get their autograph was a dream come true.

If Gavin Peacock had any real doubts about what he wanted to do when he grew up, the two years at Tampa quickly removed them. Ask him about his football heroes today and he will unhesitatingly start first with the name of Pelé. Not a surprising choice perhaps but many English players would talk about Best, Charlton or Moore. Peacock's choice reflects his introduction to world soccer at an early age and his admiration for exceptional flair and skill. Unlike many modern footballers whose sights are fixed on results, Peacock has always wanted to be a player who entertains as well as scores goals. America gave him the chance to develop his game in new ways.

'I practised quite a lot in the garden,' he recalls, 'keeping the ball up and doing different things – dribbling in and out of cones and things like that just to improve my skills. The first Sunday team I played for was a year above my age group. In my last year in America the team I played for was the best in the area and we used to win quite a few games.'

Given the choice, Gavin and Lauren would have stayed longer in America, but their father was anxious to break into management in England. Keith Peacock didn't have long to wait for his first post. Third-division Gillingham offered him a job, one he was to keep for six and a half years as one of the most popular managers in the club's modest history.

For Gavin it meant goodbye to being a schoolboy star in Tampa Bay and back to Bexley Grammar School. It must have felt like coming back to earth with a bump. For a while he was ribbed about his supposed American accent but life soon settled back into a routine.

At fourteen, the next four years of his life were dedicated to two goals – success in education and football. For many promising teenagers the opportunity of professional football is enough. Education came a poor second for Alan Comfort as soon as clubs started to show an interest. Peacock was different. His parents were well aware of the perils of trying to make it as a footballer. For every 100 schoolboys that have trials with clubs maybe only one will be offered an apprenticeship. Even then, for every batch of apprentices only a handful will eventually make the grade. Gavin Peacock had outstanding talent as a teenager but he wasn't going to be allowed to throw away his education on the strength of it. His teachers at Bexley Grammar advised him that if he worked hard then he could go on to university. If Peacock hadn't made it in football he might be a doctor today. But he had only one ambition – to follow his father and be a famous footballer.

In 1981 he remembers watching the England School-boys' game against Scotland on television. 'That could be you next year,' his dad told him. Gavin didn't really believe it. All the same he went straight out in the garden to put in a bit more practice. One year later he was walking out at Wembley.

To play for England Schoolboys in the under-fifteen side you have to go through a rigorous selection procedure which begins with regional trials around the country – each of which involves around sixty hopefuls – and leads to the cream of the crop being invited for trials at Lilleshall, the international side's training ground. To reach the final eleven you face competition from every promising fourteen year old in the land. As Keith Peacock took his seat in the crowd that day, it was a moment to compare with anything that came later.

'To see him walk out at Wembley was a tremendously proud moment. Something that I never came close to. Just to see your son walk out in front of 50,000 people and represent England as one of the eleven out of the whole country is very, very special,' he says.

Even then, education couldn't be forgotten for long. On the Saturday Gavin Peacock was playing at Wembley; on the Monday he was sitting in an exam. room pondering square roots and equations as he took his maths 'O' level one year early.

That year, Peacock played six games for England and scored twice – once against Scotland at Stoke and once against Wales at Newport. By the Scotland game at the end of the season, he was virtually the only player in the England team not to have signed for a pro-fessional club. It was not for want of interest. Evidently plenty of clubs had noticed the small dark-haired youngster with an eye for goals. Gavin Peacock could have signed for almost any London club he wished. Tottenham were in the queue along with Keith's old

club, Charlton. But again, where other teenagers might
have jumped in, Peacock talked it over carefully with
his dad. In the end they opted for Terry Venables'
Queen's Park Rangers. It was not the biggest London
club, but as the player explains, there were good reasons
for that.

'We looked at QPR and thought that they had a good
youth policy of bringing young players through into the
first team. I could have gone to Tottenham but we felt
that there were a lot more players there: you can tend
to get lost in that and I had more of a chance at QPR of
coming through.'

It was the same reasoning that drew Alan Comfort
to the Loftus Road set-up a few years earlier. Peacock
senior might have been inclined to favour his old club
Charlton, but these were not happy times at the Valley
with the club struggling to survive. Keith felt Gavin
deserved a top club. QPR, with its Astro-turf pitch and
ambitious young manager, seemed to be the club of the
future.

It was a carefully weighed decision, but the future can
never be predicted. No one knew that Terry Venables
would have barely time to shake Gavin Peacock's hand
before he boarded a plane bound for Barcelona. It was
the end of an era for the Loftus Road outfit who had
built a team to rival any of their more illustrious London
rivals. If Venables had stayed, who knows if Peacock's
career might have flourished from the start in the Premiership, as it later became. Instead, Peacock was
destined to fight his way into the top flight the hard
way.

For the moment he was glad to be part of the QPR
set-up where he trained alongside a talented young winger
called Alan Comfort. Gavin cannot recall much about their
first meetings except that they played a handful of reserve
games together. But then Alan Comfort was also soon

to move on. The next time they met, the two players would have something in common that went far beyond football.

Notes

1. George Best on 'A word with Williams' (BBC Radio).

Chapter Four

Cambridge Blues

The sports pages in the summer of 1984 were full of the departure of Terry Venables. Only at the end of the previous season Venables had pledged his future to QPR after the home game against West Bromwich Albion. But Barcelona, desperate to break the dominance of their mighty rivals Real Madrid, were offering Venables a contract said to be worth £170,000 a year. They could also boast a side which included names such as that of Diego Maradona. Rangers could not hope to compete. Exit El Tel.

Few QPR supporters would have lost much sleep over the fact that a young reserve-team winger was to leave Loftus Road soon after. Alan Comfort was nineteen – still a teenager, but one who had served eighteen months of his professional contract and was beginning to wonder if his big break would ever come.

Alan Mullery had taken over in the manager's hot seat but was finding Venables a hard act to follow. It wasn't for want of talent. Mullery had an abundance of skilful young players knocking on the first-team door. For Comfort it must have felt like standing at the back of a cinema queue wondering if the sign is going to say 'full house' by the time you reach the front.

'It was a time when you had Mike Flanagan and Ian Stewart playing in the first team, along with Wayne Fereday and Steve Burke, the former Notts. Forest player,' he recalls. 'There were four of them, all left wingers, so I don't even know how I got a game in the reserves. When it came to the crunch for the first team, if one of them wasn't fit the other one would play. They were all incredibly good players. Wayne was three years older than me and he was a lightning explosion on the football scene.'

Mullery soon decided he didn't need five players who could fill the same position. Early in the 1984–5 season he took Comfort aside to tell him that third-division Cambridge United had watched him and were interested in taking him on loan. When a player can't command a first-team place, a loan is an arrangement which can benefit all parties concerned. The player himself gets the chance to play first-team football which in the long run can only improve his value to his own club. Meanwhile he can inject some life into a lower-division team who may be short of cash to buy new players. For Alan Comfort there was nothing to lose. The loan was agreed for three weeks which amounted to seven first-team games.

At the time, Cambridge United were in the throes of an injury crisis. They were looking for someone to bolster their midfield where Steve Spriggs and Andy Sinton (the player later to cost Sheffield Wednesday £2.7 million) were both unfit. Cambridge had been a second-division outfit, and although they hadn't made a brilliant start, it was too early to say whether this might be their season. John Ryan, the manager, had been impressed with what he'd seen of Comfort. The player himself, characteristically, was excited by the prospect.

'It was my first trip away from home, the first time I had lived away properly. It was quite some drive, all the way through London up to Cambridge. I really felt that this was a very exciting change of life.'

If anybody had told Comfort just how much his life was about to change, he probably wouldn't have believed them. Certainly, Randall Butt, sports reporter on the *Cambridge Evening News*, was impressed by the newcomer's attitude:

'A young hopeful, an England youth international used to the first-division set up at Loftus Road could have been excused for feeling dismayed at being farmed out to put some meat on the bones of United's skeleton squad. But instead of the uninterested, maybe slightly arrogant young player putting up with a month in the sticks, Alan Comfort cut a very different figure. There was no mistaking the teenager's genuine enthusiasm for the move from his glamour club to Cambridge.'

Alan's long-awaited league debut came on 15 September 1984 against table-topping Bristol City at home. From the QPR reserve games watched by only a handful of fans, he was suddenly walking out in front of 6,000 supporters all eager to see if he could provide the fillip their struggling side needed. It was not Anfield with the Kop roaring in your ears, but for a nineteen year old who had spent two years waiting in the wings it was a day to remember without undue modesty.

'For any player your first league match is a big thing. But it was just like Middlesbrough later; somehow – and I'll never know how – I would produce the very best football that I was capable of. The biggest problem I had was trying to maintain the standards that the supporters suddenly hoped for.'

Comfort had a hand in both United's goals, the second crossing for Danny Greaves, son of the legendary Jimmy, to put Cambridge 2–1 up. But United faded to lose 3–2 and fall into the bottom four of the table. The other six games in the loan period tell a similar story with Cambridge

sliding to a string of defeats and Alan's exciting wing play
the only crumb of comfort for the local headline writers.

Comfort had viewed the move as a short-term experience, but John Ryan had other ideas. He was soon trying
to persuade the youngster to stay on. After the last game
of his loan, Comfort was driving home with his parents
when he saw something in a national newspaper that took
his breath away. According to the report, he had already
agreed to sign for Cambridge United.

John Ryan was under a lot of pressure to get his man
and had apparently counted on Comfort agreeing to the
deal. It left the teenager in a strong negotiating position on
Monday morning. Ryan virtually said to him, 'What can I
give you that will make you agree to sign?' It was almost a
blank cheque – an offer that might have turned the head of
any young player. Cambridge United certainly didn't have
money to throw around – they had recently been forced
to launch a 'Buy a Player' appeal among their own fans.
Nevertheless, Ryan was so eager to sign Comfort that he
agreed to double the winger's present salary and buy him
a car. An older, wiser player might still have hesitated but
looking back, Comfort thinks he was easily swayed.

'I was earning fortunes more than my father already, and
my only concept of money was how much my dad earned. I
signed and that's where I made my mistake because I may
have got that somewhere else. I signed a three-year deal
which was a massive contract. It was one that Cambridge
tried to get out of time and again as the year went on
because they gave me more money than they could really
afford.'

Today Alan Comfort sees the move to Cambridge as
the biggest mistake of his professional career. He still had
a year of his contract at QPR to run and other clubs might
have come in if his availability had become known. Unlike
Gavin Peacock he couldn't turn for advice to a father with
a long footballing career. In any case he was carried away

by his first taste of being in the spotlight; he wasn't about to ask anyone's advice.

'I didn't ask my dad if I should sign for Cambridge,' he admits. 'I didn't even ask him what he thought for the first time in my life because I wanted to make that decision. I didn't ask anyone what I should do with the manager. I was very unsure about those decisions when I made them, but I made them for the first time. That for me was very important.'

Cambridge is a city of bikes and bridges, dreaming spires and tea shops where Earl Grey and Darjeeling are still served in china cups. It is far too civilised to ever rival the hotbeds of football passion like Merseyside, Manchester or Tyneside. Yet Cambridge offered Alan Comfort the chance to become his own person. As a boy he had always felt in the shadow of his three elder sisters. To his relatives he was 'the quiet boy who played football'. Since the age of fifteen he had stayed with the same girlfriend in the sort of intense 'us against the world' relationship that only teenagers can bear. Cambridge was his ticket to freedom, and football had given him enough money to enjoy the ride.

'I bought a house outside Cambridge,' he remembers. 'It was terraced but for somebody who was nineteen it was a lovely house. I'm a homely person. I surrounded myself with nice things. I got a sports car – a Fiat X19, black with white leather seats. I only kept the car for six months because I couldn't afford the insurance; it was pushing to the limits everything I'd never been able to have.'

The car was a statement – not only to others but to himself. For the first time he felt he was in control of his life. The transfer may have been a mistake but it helped to change him from a keen-to-please teenager into someone with growing self-confidence. He was making his own decisions about the future.

It had been a new experience to sit in a manager's office knowing that he held all the trump cards in his hand.

'In every situation in my life before then I was waiting for them to say they wanted me,' he says. 'I actually asked for more to see what my worth was. That was a powerful position to be in and helped to give me much more confidence in myself. I also learnt to deal with the newspapers. At QPR everyone always talked about you as someone who "might be". Now newspapers suddenly had stories about you – your life, your football career, what you thought. After games reporters would ask, "Are you going to stay?" You held the stage.'

Stages, like football dressing-rooms, have entrances and exits. As Comfort arrived at Cambridge it was a fair bet that somebody else was on their way out. The unlucky player was Graham Daniels, a larger-than-life Welshman with the gift of the gab and a useful turn of pace on the left wing. Every football club has its characters and 'Blodwyn', as he was nicknamed among the players, stood out in many ways at Cambridge. Comfort soon noticed the Welshman.

'I used to try and work out why he was so popular with everybody,' he recalls. 'One of the reasons is that he was quite a funny guy. And he was able to talk where other people would be embarrassed. He could hold a stage. So he was an impressive person. He was sharp and he was funny in the stories he told. Everybody liked him because he was sincere. In that respect he seemed different.'

There was something else unusual about Daniels. He was religious, 'a Christian', the other players warned Comfort with knowing looks.

Graham Daniels had come into football late at the age of twenty-one. Unlike most players, who leave school at sixteen to start an apprenticeship, Daniels had gone on to university where he had combined football for Cardiff City with a philosophy of religion degree. This alone would

have made him different. But in the last year Daniels'
interest in religion had become more than academic. The
high point of his playing career had come in a match against
Newcastle at St James's Park. On the opposing side was his
boyhood hero Kevin Keegan. He has never forgotten the
occasion.

'To me it was a dream come true; everything I'd always
wanted was encapsulated in that one match. I scored. We
lost 2–1 but I scored. It was all those emotions that are
good in football that night and the next day. But then
that old feeling that football had often brought me – the
Monday morning feeling. So what next?'

Daniels didn't even have the satisfaction of seeing his
moment of glory in print. By a cruel irony the Sunday
papers were cancelled the next day because of a strike.
Feeling that even soccer's glory moments were not enough,
he started to look into Christianity. When Alan Comfort
arrived at Cambridge, Daniels had been a Christian for
only a few months.

As far as Comfort was concerned, Graham Daniels was
simply the player he had been bought to replace. It seems
everyone at the club was aware of this except Graham
Daniels himself. He remembers first meeting the new boy
in a midweek practice match.

'He arrived for training – just another new lad. But he
looked really good, a cut above us, so it was obvious he'd
come from a higher level. So I asked someone, "Do you
know who the new lad is?" They said, "Oh he's from QPR;
he's a midfield player."'

To Daniels, who played on the left wing, this news was
a great relief. He even began to think how the two of
them would make a good combination on the left side of
the field. But when he spoke to Comfort he discovered
that the manager had something else in mind. He replays
the conversation in his soft Welsh accent, rolling his eyes
comically:

"So you play left-hand side of midfield?"

'He said, "Yeah, but I'm a winger really."

'And I thought, "Oh no, nowaa!"'

On Comfort's part there wasn't much room for senti-
ment. Football is a fiercely competitive world. No player
can ever rest secure in the knowledge that his place is safe.
There are only eleven names on the teamsheet on Saturday
so someone is always going to be disappointed. Naturally
enough, Alan didn't get too close to the Welshman at
first. He remembers thinking, 'I don't know if I can have
a relationship with him as a person because I'm just taking
his job and I have no intention of letting him have it back.
He represented the opposition. I'm sure that he would
have felt the same about me in some ways.'

Daniels was certainly struggling with mixed emotions.
As a Christian he felt he ought to be friendly to the
youngster just up from the big city. But as a footballer
it was gradually dawning on him that his job was on the
line. Alan Comfort's arrival not only meant he was out
of the team. In the long run it could mean he was out of
football for good.

From mid-September to Christmas, the name of Comfort repeatedly appeared on the teamsheet while Daniels
watched from the stands or occasionally got onto the subs
bench. The Welshman talks about his feelings at the time
with refreshing honesty.

'You sit in the stand during a game and the team
does well and you're disappointed because you know you
won't get in next week. Or the team wins and the guy in
your place doesn't do so well and you're really pleased.
Obviously as a person, and as a Christian, you'd think,
"I know this is a bad emotion but to contain it is virtually
impossible."'

To his Cambridge team-mates it became increasingly
clear that Graham Daniels could be finished in football.
A footballer whose career is about to end at the age of

twenty-four is like someone who's been told he's only got a few months to live. This may sound an exaggeration but in professional sport success is everything. Football clubs thrive on an optimism bordering on insanity. Every Saturday players must believe that they'll win, every season that they'll get promotion, every year that their career can reach greater heights. Football's lifeblood is a belief in tomorrow. A player staring the end of his career in the face at twenty-four is like having someone dressed for his own funeral in the changing room. It would have been natural for players to start avoiding Graham Daniels. But the problem was, he refused to act like someone whose life was about to fall apart. This was what bothered Alan Comfort. He could accept that Daniels was different from other players in many ways – witty, articulate and intelligent – but why wasn't he responding to his personal crisis in the normal way? His wife was expecting a baby and he was about to lose his job and his livelihood. Yet still he went on insisting that God cared about him. So where was his God when he needed him most?

'At that point we began to ask him basic questions,' says Comfort. 'Survival questions. Does God help you survive or not? If you are telling us we should believe in him, give us the evidence. It was a general question that seventeen people were asking him in different ways, not just me.'

Graham Daniels didn't pretend to have all the answers. All he could offer was an unshakeable faith that God hadn't given up on him.

'There were times when I'd go home and I'd be so fed up that I wasn't in the first team,' he recalls. 'Yet in all that I had a security that it would be okay. Whatever happened it would be okay. Someone might say, "Aren't you worried?" And I would say, "Yes, I'm apprehensive – but not worried. I'm convinced that God's in charge and he wants the best for me."'

It was this that impressed the nineteen year old who had

been bought to replace him. It was as if Alan Comfort looked in a mirror and saw himself at the end of his playing days. Football had been the focus of his whole life since childhood, but now the question arose, what was left after football had gone?

'I knew I'd play football for ten, fifteen years at the most. But he had hold of something that was more important than what I was doing,' says Comfort. 'I now had the money to go out and buy things and I could also play football. I felt important as a person because I had everything. But seeing Daniels, I think I realised that there was something more important even than football. It was life – how you actually live your life. I could remember times that I had been questioning, "Is all my life going to be about money, football, being able to buy another house, another car? Am I just going to be moving up a ladder and striving to do that?" Realising that the ladder I had climbed so far had made no difference to me as a person inside, I didn't feel any better about myself. What he represented was not success materially, not even a direction in life. What he represented was a person who had found something more important.'

Probably everyone in their lives asks these kind of questions at some point. 'Is this it? Is this what life comes down to?' The question may not be directed at God, and certainly Alan Comfort wouldn't have classed himself as 'religious' – he had never been to church in his life. Even at his sister's wedding he missed the service and only made the reception because of a football match. But as a teenager he had always been on the lookout for answers. Once a visiting speaker had come to an RE class at school and talked about God. Comfort was the only one in his class who had fired question after question. At the end, the speaker invited him to hear a talk at the church that evening. He didn't go. Like most teenagers he felt it would have been too embarrassing.

A few years later, at the age of seventeen and with the doors to professional football wide open to him, he found himself knocking on the door of a church. It was a midweek afternoon and no one was around to answer.

'Basically I'd stood at the door saying, "God if you are there . . ." But I felt so embarrassed when the door wasn't open. I thought, "What am I trying to find here?" I had no answers.'

Those two moments in life had passed him by. But now, just as his career was taking off, the questions were back again. And they demanded to be answered. Comfort admits that he secretly hoped that Graham Daniels would come in one day and confess that he'd got the whole thing wrong. 'My need to see him fail was enormous,' he says. But Daniels clung doggedly to his faith that God had a plan for his life and would look after him. The younger player was drawn as if to a magnet. It wasn't that he wanted to be Graham Daniels – far from it – but he wanted to know what he had. He was filled with a desire, a compulsion to find out.

'People had always said, "This is how you live. You enjoy it while it lasts. So you have your football career, you don't know for how long but you enjoy it while it lasts." Daniels was somebody whom time had run out on as far as I could see. Nobody had ever given me the other half of the answer. If you enjoy it while it lasts, I could only think that when it ended there was nothing. There was no answer to that, you were just sad and sorry. He gave a different answer. His answer was, "I've got something that this football career can't take away. The most precious thing you can have in life is this relationship with God."'

Something had to happen. It was as if Alan Comfort was just waiting for someone to light the blue touch-paper inside him. In the end it happened without any accompanying fireworks.

Daniels recalls, 'I asked him to come to a youth club because we were showing *The Cross and the Switchblade* on a Friday night (a film about an American gang leader who becomes a Christian). When we got back to my house afterwards, we talked about the film and what he thought. I said to him, "You'll really need to think about becoming a Christian yourself at this rate." And he said (he's quite straight to the point, Alan, he calls a spade a spade), "Oh I have."

'"What do you mean you have?"

'"I have tonight. I made up my mind I'm going to be a Christian."'

Three days later, Alan Comfort went to a prayer meeting for the first time in his life. It was at a Brethren church in Cambridge. He remembers just one thing from the evening – that half way through a man got up to speak.

'As he spoke it was as if I saw my life in sharp focus for the first time. There was this frustrating sense of being trapped. I wanted to be free to live my life but somehow I always seemed to end up disappointing myself and others. Even the people I loved most – my girlfriend, Sue, and my family – seemed to let me down. I wasn't looking for some kind of wonder drug. I wanted something solid, the truth. And this man seemed to be speaking about the most incredible answer. As he talked about Jesus dying on a cross to carry the sin of every person, the peace I had seen in Graham started to make sense. I found myself asking God to forgive me. Immediately I felt free, as if a huge burden had been lifted from my shoulders.'

As Alan Comfort left the church that night he knew his life had changed direction once and for all. He had no regrets about the change but there were more than a few questions to be answered. How was someone like him, who had never been to church in his life, going to fit in? Even more daunting, what would be the reaction of his family and Sue when he told them? And what about his team-mates? They would have to be faced – and sooner rather than later.

Some people might have waited for the right opportunity or spoken to individual players in a quiet way. Alan Comfort is not that kind of person. He decided the only thing was to announce to his team-mates that he'd become a Christian in the dressing room the next day. The reaction was not overwhelming.

'There was a silence, just a silence. I knew that it wasn't going to be, "Well why have you done that?" I knew that the questions wouldn't come out. At that moment it was important for me to say something.'

Whatever the players thought, they kept it to themselves at the time. Comfort was nineteen and still the new boy to them. Graham Daniels was the only Christian they knew and so they probably laughed among themselves at 'Blodwyn's disciple'.

In any case, there were other things to worry about than an outbreak of religion in the Cambridge squad. The team were firmly rooted at the bottom of division three and showing no signs of hauling themselves out of the mire. A home game against Burnley in November summed up their season. With manager John Ryan making his home debut to try and shore up his team's leaky defence, Cambridge were two goals up by half-time – Steve Spriggs volleying home from a Comfort cross for the first. But then the old capacity to pluck defeat from the jaws of victory returned. Burnley pulled a goal back and in the sixty-third minute Cambridge's player manager caught the ball in his hands to cut out a dangerous pass. He had been booked once and promptly received his marching orders. Ryan must have wished he could have climbed into an early bath like other players. Instead he was forced to sit on the bench and watch his ten-man team as Burnley came back to win 3–2.

An FA Cup exit at the hands of fourth-division Peterborough followed, and the odds looked against the Cambridge manager celebrating a happy Christmas. He was sent off again for swearing at the referee in a match with Lincoln.

It was a staggering four and a half months before Alan Comfort played in a winning Cambridge side in front of the home fans. The occasion was not a big one – the first leg of the Freight Rover trophy against Peterborough, but at least Comfort had the satisfaction of scoring an amazing goal. He collected the ball by the touchline on the left flank and curled it right-footed into the far top corner of the net. 'I only use the right leg for standing on usually,' he joked afterwards.

Looking back, Alan remembers his first season with Cambridge as an unsettling period. 'As a young player coming in, it was all very exciting in the beginning, but we kept losing. The manager came under more and more pressure. When the pressure's on, people panic and they begin to believe that the people they've signed have let them down. I was nineteen years old and here was a man who was thinking that I was going to win them games. I learnt very quickly about football that one player doesn't win anything for anybody; it takes a team. The team just couldn't do it. My memory of that first period is that my confidence as a footballer was gradually drained. If you keep losing you lose your confidence. Then I was dropped at one time and missed a few games, then came back, then got dropped again. It only ever happened in my Cambridge career.'

For any young player it would have been a traumatic introduction into professional football, but the storms on the field were nothing in comparison to what was happening in Comfort's personal life. His decision to become a committed Christian had ushered in a sea change in his life. Not everyone was to welcome the disturbance.

Chapter Five

A Different Ballgame

'We all knew from the start he was going to be brilliant,' says Alan Comfort of the newest arrival at QPR in 1984. Gavin Peacock was still not quite seventeen, but there was already something that marked him out as a player for the future.

'I'm a confidence player,' explains Comfort. 'If the crowd booed I'd miss the ball. But Gavin has a confidence within. That's something very special in a footballer. It means he can survive the football world with fewer ups and downs.'

It is an accurate assessment. Peacock's career was to have its fair share of downs later – he came close to being relegated with different clubs three times in the space of four seasons. But his confidence in his own ability never wavered. Most players will admit their own game is greatly affected by the form of the team they play for. Gavin Peacock has always had the happy knack of performing well and scoring goals even when the rest of the side is struggling. When Newcastle United flirted dangerously with relegation in the 1991–2 season, Peacock's name was on the scoresheet twenty-one times.

Where does that sort of unshakeable confidence come

from? Early success may have had something to do with it – from the start he was always the outstanding player at school and went on to the recognition of England Schoolboys. But plenty of other hopefuls reached the same heights only to fade into obscurity later. Gavin Peacock's confidence as a player more likely stems from a self-assurance that is the bedrock of his personality. It is as evident when he is talking to 'Sports Report' on BBC Radio as when he walks onto a football field. At twenty-five he gives the impression of a person at ease with himself and the world.

If you believe psychologists, childhood has an enormous effect on character and personality in later life. Peacock is fortunate that his family background gave him a headstart. Not only did he have a secure childhood, he had a family that was unusually close and supportive. Even today, if you're at Stamford Bridge to watch Chelsea, it is likely that Gavin Peacock's mother, father, sister or wife (or all of them) will be somewhere in the crowd cheering him on. It is something that he readily acknowledges means a lot to him.

'It's always been the case that mum and dad and family are there, and that has been a rock to lean on all the time. Obviously I'm my own person now, but my family's always there to lean on if needed. That has been something very important in my life. That stability and strength that comes from a family.'

There is another kind of rock which has helped him to cope with the ups and downs of life. But as a seventeen year old turning pro. with Queen's Park Rangers, religion wasn't something that Peacock gave much thought to. He was too busy trying to make his mark at a club that could boast such seasoned professionals as John Gregory and Terry Fenwick.

Peacock wasn't the biggest or chunkiest player on the staff at the time. Even today he stands only five foot eight

inches tall and weighs a slim eleven stone. What he lacks
in stature he makes up for in ability and enthusiasm. It
is typical of him that he started his first day's training
at QPR like an express train trying to break all speed
records. Most footballers will tell you that pre-season
training, with its hard physical regime of sprints, stretches
and press-ups, is the worst part of being a professional. A
smaller-than-average seventeen year old in his first season
needs time to adjust, as Peacock found out to his cost.

'I was flying around everywhere in training. I thought
I had to run everywhere and I never stopped running. I
put it all in the first day and some of the older pros were
saying, "There's four more weeks of this to go. Steady
down, calm down." But I was trying to be all enthusiastic
and run around. In the car coming home I went to get out
and my hamstring just cramped up: I couldn't move.'

The two older players who were in the car to wit-
ness his agony were Gary Micklewhite and Steve Burke.
Predictably they were too busy laughing to offer any help.
They soon found other ways to have a laugh at the new
boy's expense.

'They used to catch me all the time on different tricks,'
remembers Peacock. 'Going over Westminster Bridge
they'd say, "What's the time Gavin?" And I'd say, "Oh
it's nine-thirty." And they'd both start laughing because
there was Big Ben right in front of me.'

Football clubs thrive on such practical jokes. On a big
match day, when nerves are on edge, it's vital that each
team has its resident comedian to ease the tension. It
is said that Graham Taylor employed his ex-Watford
assistant Steve Harrison with the England International
set-up partly because he was a great practical joker
who could get players laughing and relaxing together.
Unfortunately for Harrison he went one joke too far
while at Millwall and lost his job both at club and
international level.

Another man who wasn't seeing the funny side of football in the 1984–5 season was Alan Mullery. The ex-Spurs and England player had taken over from Venables in 1984 but his affair with the Loftus Road club was to be brief and torrid. Mullery in those days, eyes shaded by tinted glasses and mouth compulsively chewing gum, presented the strongest argument for football management being the worst job in the world. He sat hunched and restless on the bench as his team slumped to a series of defeats. You could almost hear the knives being sharpened in the boardroom. It was no surprise when he got the sack before the season was out. If the seventeen-year-old Gavin Peacock needed any reminder that football was an unpredictable business, Mullery provided it.

But Peacock's future was about to change in ways that had nothing to do with football. He had life at his feet: a contract with a top first-division club, ten 'O' levels if he ever needed to pursue another career, and no shortage of girlfriends (although none of them lasted long if they made the mistake of getting too serious). Most seventeen year olds would have felt that life was shaping up nicely and Peacock was no exception. Unlike Alan Comfort – who by this time had moved on to Cambridge – he had no burning questions about life. It was simply that something stepped in at this point and demanded an answer. The person who started it all was his mother, Leslie Peacock.

Leslie Peacock met her future husband at the age of eleven. 'It was love at first sight in the playground,' she laughs. Their first date came when she was fifteen and Keith was sixteen. Like most teenage couples in those days they arranged to meet at the cinema. But it wasn't until the Pathé newsreel, with highlights of the weekend's football, that Leslie had any inkling that there was another passion in her boyfriend's life.

'He was on the edge of his chair, not paying any attention to me,' she says. 'I didn't realise that he was so into it. I said to him, "Do you like football?" and he said, "Just a bit."

'He used to play for the school team. He used to play everything because he was an all-round sportsman; he was in the rugby team and the cricket team. So I didn't think too much about it. It wasn't until we'd been going out for a few weeks that he said he wanted to be a professional footballer. But it meant nothing to me. Being an only child I didn't have any brothers or sisters to take me to football; my father wasn't a football person.'

Keith was already playing for Charlton Colts. As soon as he reached seventeen he signed for the Valley club. Two years later, in 1965, the couple were married. At first they lived in a club house paying £1.50 a week rent all in. At that time many footballers stayed in club houses because of the uncertainty of the transfer market, but the Peacocks decided to take the risk of buying. It paid off – Keith was to stay at Charlton for seventeen years.

Gavin was born two years into the marriage. From an early age it was Leslie who took him to watch his father play at Charlton. Football took her husband away on traditional family days such as Easter, Christmas and New Year, but against this Keith would be home on most afternoons. Looking back, Leslie thinks the family gained more than they lost from football.

'Keith and I together could spend so much time with the children when they were young as opposed to my contemporaries who had nine-to-five jobs. They'd come home, the children might be in bed or they might see them for an hour. There was so much we could share. I think that possibly all this time we were able to spend together in the early years was what helped to mould us into a close family. I would say we are very, very close.'

Closeness included the occasional trip to church, but only for weddings, christenings or special events like Christmas.

Sunday school never stood much chance because Gavin played football on Sundays.

Leslie had been educated in a convent school until the age of twelve but lapsed in practising her faith once she got to secondary school. Nevertheless, she'd retained a strong belief in God and felt that some day she ought to do something about it. The time arrived in 1986, during Gavin's second year at QPR.

'I'd been thinking about it for a long time and thinking that life had been very good to me,' she says. 'Youth had rushed by and it was like one hadn't had time for God, hadn't had time for Christianity. I felt that was wrong and that I should do something about it; that what I should do is go and get confirmed and make a commitment to say "Thank you". I've found myself, like most people, very quick to pray and ask and very slow to pray to thank.'

She got in touch with her local minister at the Methodist church. They talked about confirmation classes and a lot more besides. According to the minister, Christianity involved more than belief in God, prayers and leading a moral life. There was a decision to be made involving a commitment to follow Christ with your whole life.

It was a new version of Christianity as far as Leslie Peacock was concerned. Gavin remembers well the first time he discussed the subject with his mother, after her return from church.

'She came back one day and she said she'd become a Christian. I said, "Well, what does that mean? I thought I was a Christian." She said no – that she'd made a commitment to God and asked God into her life to be the centre of it. She felt different.

'I didn't think much of it but I seemed to see a change in her in the next few weeks. Things that used to upset her didn't. She had a happier outlook on things and said she felt closer to God and had more of a personal relationship with him. She was praying and felt that he was here around her. Things in the Bible were coming to life; she understood them all of a sudden.'

Many teenagers would have dismissed it but Gavin was interested and his curiosity deepened when his mother abruptly quit smoking.

Leslie says, 'I had been a very heavy smoker and one day I just prayed to God and asked him to help me stop smoking. I said, "That's it. I'm not having another one" – and I didn't. I didn't touch another one for three and a half years. What amazed everybody was the ease with which I did it. I can say in complete honesty that from the minute I prayed, I stopped. I never wanted or craved another cigarette again.

'Gavin, along with everyone else, was absolutely astounded. My mother and mother-in-law smoke, and they'd say, "Does it bother you?" I'd say, "Not in the least." Because I'm not a very disciplined person, they thought, "That's it; she's obviously had help from someone else."'

Gavin agrees that he was impressed.

'It impressed everyone in the family. It was the reality of God I think that was the big thing. I'd always believed God was there but there was no personal touch. But now he was affecting someone that I was living with – my mum, and it was affecting her in a real way. So I felt that was what I wanted, that reality of God.'

He decided he would go along to the church to see for himself. The congregation was far from the few old ladies in hats that he expected to find at a service. There were a lot of people of his own age who attended a youth group at the minister's house after the Sunday evening service. Gavin felt they had something that he didn't. 'They used to speak about God, about Jesus as if they knew him personally, as if he was a personal friend.'

Within a few weeks he decided it was something he wanted. He became a Christian. There was no dramatic turning point as with Alan Comfort. It was simply a very definite decision that he wanted to know God in his life.

His mother didn't find the news surprising.

'No, I wasn't surprised because this was typical Gavin. He doesn't do things by halves. When he takes an interest and wants to go into something he goes all the way. I think it's been really great for him. I've seen a change in him. He's always been a nice lad, but it helped him to become a more complete person.'

On Gavin's part he felt his new faith bred a confidence and contentment that wasn't there before. 'It was exciting; suddenly I wasn't alone all the time. I could talk to God whenever I wanted and he knew my problems. He knew all I was going through at work or wherever. It wasn't just down to me to make my own way. I take it as a consequence that my football came on a lot as well.'

As far as QPR were concerned, Peacock was showing more than useful progress. In his second season he was already knocking on the first-team door. Following Alan Mullery's departure, Frank Sibley had seen out the 1984–5 season as caretaker manager. The next season Jim Smith arrived.

'The Bald Eagle' is one of the game's most colourful managers. He has had spells at Oxford, QPR, Newcastle and Portsmouth. He was to figure twice as manager in Gavin Peacock's career, the second time at Tyneside. Peacock remembers that he was warned by his dad that Smith was a 'bit of a growler'. Stories about Smith's explosive temper are legendary in football. Chairman Robert Maxwell once sat in the dug-out with him to see the Oxford manager at work. The burly newspaper tycoon only lasted ten minutes before the torrent of cursing and swearing forced him to return to his seat in the director's box. Peacock got the sharp end of the new manager's tongue on one or two occasions but Smith must have seen something he liked because he included the seventeen year old on a pre-season friendly trip.

Peacock found himself on the coach with first-team players like Terry Fenwick, Gary Waddock, Mike Fillory, Alan McDonald and John Gregory, an England international. The youngster knew he was only along for the ride and still expected to lay out the kit and carry the balls for training, but that didn't diminish the thrill of knowing he was good enough to be there.

His chance came in a friendly against Fulham where he came on as substitute for half an hour. Immediately after the game he telephoned his dad to tell him the news. That season might have seen his first-team debut but for the fact that he got glandular fever around Christmas and was out for three months at a crucial stage of the season.

Early in the 1986–7 season, Peacock, with the new-found confidence of his faith, was showing useful form in midfield. Smith himself took the young player aside to tell him he wasn't far off his first-team debut. It was all the incentive he needed to give everything in reserve-team games. Shortly after his nineteenth birthday he was handed the present he'd been waiting for: he was in the team to face Sheffield Wednesday that Saturday.

Talk to any professional footballer and they'll probably remember their league debut alongside other landmarks in their career. The chance came for Alan Comfort in front of around 6,000 people at Cambridge United. Gavin Peacock was coming in at the top – a (former) first-division match in front of a crowd of around 15,000 home supporters. Among them were his mother, sister, grandparents and the headmaster from his old school (Keith Peacock missed his son's debut because he was managing Gillingham). To the rest of the crowd Peacock G. was just an unfamiliar name on the back of the programme. For the player himself it was the moment he'd been building up to for the last five years. As he pulled on the blue-hooped shirt in the dressing-room, he tried not to think about the next ninety minutes. Would he be a hero or a disaster? Score on his debut or put through his own goal? The pre-match nerves were much worse than anything that could happen on the pitch.

'I was in the dressing-room with all those experienced pros.,' he says. 'They all try and calm you down and just say play your normal game and you'll be all right once you get out there. I think most pros. are like that: they'll try and help younger players, especially if someone is making his debut, even though they're on the line themselves and wanting to do well.

'It was quite stressful, the atmosphere. Beforehand you are nervous and it builds up. And then during the game the crowd fades into the background for me. The crowd's there but you're in your own world. You're concentrating on the game. Obviously you hear them when you're going forward – the roar – and when you've had a shot, but it's not the same as before.'

In the event he came close to making a sensational start on the infamous Astro turf.

'I nearly scored after about ten minutes. I had a diving header and it just went past the post. I did all right. I had a decent game. I got cramp and came off towards the end. I remember it flying by very quickly. I remember it being fast. Sheffield Wednesday were a bit more direct in those days, a bit more of a "knock it long team". But it was definitely faster. And of course a lot of nervous energy was being burnt up which probably made me more tired at the end. The crowd gave me a clap. I think they thought I was all right.'

The game ended in a 2–2 draw with Rangers throwing away a two-goal lead. One good game didn't mean a guaranteed place, and in the next match Peacock found himself back on the subs. bench against Arsenal. That season he was in and out of the first team playing twelve games and scoring once. The occasion of his first league goal was memorable for all the wrong reasons. Again Sheffield Wednesday were the opposition, but this time they trounced QPR 7–1. 'I've been a Sheffield Wednesday fan all my life,' Rangers' manager Jim Smith told reporters afterwards. 'The rest of what I want to say is unprintable.'

The season was a lesson in the switchback world of professional football. One week Peacock might be playing in front of 15–20,000 supporters and shaking hands with England skipper Bryan Robson. The next game it was back to the ghostly terraces of a reserve game.

But the season ended on a high note. Peacock received a letter saying he'd been selected for an England under-nineteen tour of South America. To be picked for a tour by England manager Bobby Robson, along with stars of the future such as Paul Ince, Paul Merson and David Hurst, was an honour in itself. To be playing in South America, home of the legendary Brazilians, made it doubly special.

Peacock had to be content with being sub. for the Brazil match and playing against a Uruguay representative eleven, but he has vivid memories of the trip. They stayed in Rio de Janeiro, the vast sprawling city where children sleep in cardboard boxes within a few miles of the luxurious homes of the rich. The England players were subject to an eleven o'clock curfew, and unlike Alan Comfort, Peacock was careful not to break it. There were other hazards to be wary of. Peacock remembers that in such a poverty-stricken area, prostitution and theft were commonplace.

'We were warned not to take anything on the beach because they (the thieves) had this trick. They'd straighten out a coathanger with the hook on the end and slide it under the sand where you were lying and hook your handbag or your wallet away while you were sunbathing or sleeping.'

For Bobby Robson the trip must have been a welcome break from the pressures of the full international side. At the time Robson was suffering the usual ritual abuse of England managers. Ever since 1966, when Alf Ramsey made the mistake of winning the World Cup, the England job has been a poisoned chalice for every manager who has taken it.

It was cruelly said of Robson 'that his indecision was final,' but Gavin Peacock is not one to join in the criticism. He remembers Robson as a 'very genuine, patriotic person. He always drummed home the honour and the importance of playing for your country and who you were actually representing. There was a great sense of pride about his job and what he was trying to do.

'I felt sorry for the way he was treated in the press, but that's happened to every England manager. They stick the knife in and if they take a dislike to someone then you can't do anything about it.

'I saw him a year ago. We played Sporting Lisbon (Robson's team) in a friendly tournament up at Newcastle. I went up to him and said, "You might not remember me." He said, "Oh yes, I remember you," and asked about my dad because he knows him. I scored against Sporting Lisbon that day. I got in between two players and scored a header. And Bobby was saying, "I was had by the smallest player on the pitch."'

Peacock is quick to point out that he wasn't in fact the smallest player on the pitch, but there aren't many players at five foot eight who score as often with their head. Peacock is reminiscent in that sense of his boss at Newcastle, Kevin Keegan, who seemed to grow another five inches whenever he got in the opposing penalty area.

1986 was memorable for Peacock's debut at QPR, but also for another reason. It was the year he first met Amanda, the girl he was later to marry. The setting wasn't a party or a nightclub; only a footballer like

Peacock could have met his wife at a History evening class.

Although he had signed professional at seventeen, Peacock wasn't finished with education. In his first season he had gone to night school to take English 'A' level, often reading his class books on the train into work. Young players can get an education grant from the PFA towards course work, but Peacock admits he wouldn't have been inclined to discuss his studies with other players in the dressing-room.

'I didn't let the lads know too much what I was reading,' he grins. 'I used to have Shakespeare and then I'd bring out *The Sun* newspaper when I got to work!' Prompted by his parents, he aimed to gain two 'A' levels by the time he was eighteen so that he would have the same educational qualifications as someone who had stayed on at school. As it turned out, he passed English but failed History. 1986 found him back in night school.

He arrived late for the first class and sat down opposite a girl around his own age who had long dark hair and an open, attractive face.

'We just got on really well from the start,' says Gavin. 'We used to sit together and when we had a break I'd chat to her about different things. I felt I could talk to her about anything.'

Amanda's first impressions were more definite. She claims she knew from that first meeting that she wanted to go out with Gavin – even that he was the person she would one day marry. After their first meeting that night she remembers going home and telling her mum all about him.

For the next few weeks the two sat together in the class and chatted over tea breaks. Amanda discovered her new classmate was a footballer. This didn't impress her much because she knew nothing about football. Yet he wasn't the flashy 'Jack the Lad' type she'd imagined a footballer would be. She was attracted by his easy manner and self-assurance and soon found history lessons were enlivened by his sense of humour. Over a cup of tea one evening he mentioned that he was a Christian and she laughed, thinking it might be another joke.

'I laughed because you don't imagine a footballer and a Christian go together. I didn't really ask him much about it at that stage. I wasn't sure I believed him. I suppose I had the stereotyped image that a Christian is someone who wears spectacles, is very boring, doesn't have a good time anywhere. You didn't see them as fun-loving people, as normal.'

At the end of the year, Gavin ironically missed the exam because of the England trip to South America, but it was Amanda who suggested they keep in touch. There was no question of them going out together. At that stage they were both seeing other people. Amanda admits that she would have 'jumped into a relationship right there and then' but Gavin wanted to keep things on a friendship basis. 'At that time he was a confirmed bachelor,' she says. 'He had a few girlfriends but didn't imagine himself marrying until he was twenty-eight or thirty. He had no interest in settling down.'

Gavin agrees. 'I never really had a serious relationship. I didn't fancy it. When the girls got a bit heavy into seeing you too much, I would call it a day.'

His reluctance to get too involved meant that he and Amanda remained 'just good friends' for two years. They would meet occasionally at Gavin's house or to go to the pictures, but both felt free to go out with other people. But during this period a change took place in Amanda.

When she first went to church she frankly admits it was only as an extra day in the week that she could see Gavin. But gradually, as she began attending the youth group on Sunday evenings, she started to find other reasons.

'Everybody was so kind, so very interested in you as a

person,' she recalls. 'It was something that I'd never really experienced before. My parents are divorced and I'd been through a rough time with that. I'd been reading about transcendental meditation and all kinds of religions with a friend, so I suppose I was looking for something but I didn't realise that Christianity might be it.'

After the first youth group she remembers writing in her diary: 'I've come home.' Nevertheless, it took a year until she felt she had separated Gavin from her desire to know God and was ready to become a Christian herself. At that time she was working in Sussex as a live-in nanny and committed her life to God on a train journey home.

'I didn't feel anything,' she recalls. 'No flashes of light or anything you'd expect. I got home and felt a bit disappointed. But when I went to bed that night I felt God saying to me, "You prayed once and you don't need to pray again." It was like someone inviting you to dinner and you keep saying, "Are you *sure* it's okay to come?"'

That was at Easter 1987. By November the next year the couple were no longer just friends. The change was due on Gavin's part to a growing awareness that the girl he really wanted to spend time with was his best friend.

'I think Amanda was a bit scared because she thought if it doesn't work out it might break our friendship up,' says Gavin. 'But I'd been going out with lots of other girls and each time I seemed to think, "Well I like Amanda better than any of the others."'

Amanda's conversion to Christianity had brought the two closer together. They now shared a common motivation in life. With other girlfriends Gavin had felt the relationship always reached a certain level before hitting an emotional roadblock; at that point he would quickly cool things off. Amanda was the first girl he could talk with of his desire to know God. In late 1986 Gavin Peacock wrote in his diary that he'd met a girl at night school whom he felt he could get quite close to. By February 1989, only four months after they started going out, Amanda and Gavin got engaged.

While life and love were blossoming, on the football field things had run into an unexpected siding. After a taste of first-team football, Peacock expected the 1987–8 season to be the one where he established himself as a regular at QPR. Things didn't go to plan. Under Jim Smith, Rangers had their best start to the season in a long time. They sat proudly on the top of the (old) first division for over two months. Peacock meanwhile spent much of his time sitting frustrated on the substitutes' bench. Smith had spent over a million pounds on players like Paul Parker, Dean Towley and Kevin Brock. He was playing a new sweeper system which was bringing results and there wasn't a place for the twenty year old in an experienced, successful side.

It happens all the time in football: a young player is kept waiting in the wings as cover to keep in reserve. Alan Comfort left QPR because he could see no room for himself in the position he played. Peacock in contrast felt his versatility – he had played both in midfield and upfront – was counting against him.

'I was playing for the reserves and playing quite well – having to play well just to get my place on the bench for the first team. Although it was nice to be involved with a side that was winning games, I was getting on for the last ten or fifteen minutes of games and I was a bit frustrated because I wanted to play regularly. I'd had a little taste of first-team football and I felt I needed it. And in the reserves I was playing a lot up front and I wanted to play in midfield. I wouldn't have minded if I was being played in midfield and groomed for a certain position, but I didn't feel I was. I felt I needed to get somewhere.'

Peacock wanted first-team football today not tomorrow, but QPR weren't prepared to guarantee it. The chance had to come from elsewhere. As it turned out, it came from a source sitting just across the breakfast table.

Chapter Six

On the Line

To have one Christian at a professional football club is unusual, to have two is an epidemic. The New Year of 1985 was one of the most exciting times in Alan Comfort's life. Some people arrive at faith by gradual stages, but he had encountered Christianity like a man stumbling on a treasure in a field. Overnight it had revolutionised his whole outlook on life. During those first months it was like walking around with a fire burning inside him.

'I could hardly contain myself,' he says. 'God was inside me, in my head, in my heart. I know it sounds strange to someone who hasn't experienced it, but it was happening. I found myself talking to God all the time ('praying' they told me), asking him to be with me in everything I did and to change me so people would want what I had.'

Inside he felt liberated and he might have expected his football to blossom as a result. The opposite happened. Where Gavin Peacock's faith bred a new confidence in his ability, Comfort was finding it hard to keep his mind on his game. Professional football demands total commitment and dedication from its players. Any disruption of routine and motivation can be a disaster. Comfort regretfully admits that from the day he became a Christian his football career took a back seat for several months. During the remainder of the season he was a frustrating enigma for the Cambridge United management and supporters. 'Bags of talent but no consistency' must have been the verdict from the terraces. None of the fans could have guessed what was going on inside their young winger. The fact was, he needed space and time to work out what had happened to him.

Sadly for Cambridge United, time was something they were running short of. By February relegation clouds were gathering over the club, now lying sixteen points adrift from safety in division three. As the *Cambridge Evening News* reported: 'United are trapped in a vicious circle, needing results to restore faith and belief but looking so bereft of confidence that it is difficult to see where their next win could possibly come from.'

But if faith and belief were lacking on the field, they were certainly issues very much at stake in the dressing-room. Graham Daniels was an influential character in the Cambridge playing staff and now he had been joined by another Christian. God was very much on the agenda. It was a time of heated debate at the club – not everyone was as enthusiastic about Christianity as Daniels and Comfort.

One player – who shall remain nameless – started a one-man hate campaign against what he saw as the religious disease spreading through the team. He would come into the ground early every morning and sit in his car, going through the morning papers. From these he cut out any headlines that dealt with religious hypocrisy such as 'Vicar in Love Triangle'. He would pin the cuttings up on the club noticeboard and say, 'Look at that. That's what your lot are like.'

This went on for some weeks until an incident which shook both Alan Comfort and Graham Daniels. It came after a game where both players had been in the side (Daniels had been recalled as a makeshift left back in an injury crisis). The following week they were called into the manager's office together to see John Ryan. It was not to congratulate them on their form – Ryan informed them he was placing them both on the transfer list. When asked for his reasons, he explained that he had been talking to one or two managers who had warned him that a Christian can be a bad influence on the rest of the side. Ryan was obviously a worried man. His team were struggling and his job was on the line. He was easily convinced that this religious business might be partly to blame – maybe his players had other things on their mind than the next game. He added that he had also had complaints that there was too much talk about Christianity in the dressing-room.

Comfort and Daniels were amazed and indignant. They had made no secret of their beliefs, but they had also been careful not to push them uninvited on other players. From the start they agreed never to initiate conversations about Christianity with other players. If someone asked questions then they were not backward in answering, but the rule was that they never made the first move. No one likes to have religion forced down their throat and in any case, they were employed as professional footballers not evangelists.

All this they pointed out to John Ryan who gave them a fair hearing. They denied the allegations as unfair and untrue. Shouldn't they be given the chance to speak to the players and discover the source of the complaints?

Ryan, to his credit, gave them permission. He explained the situation to the players and then shut the dressing-room door, leaving Daniels and Comfort to say their piece. The atmosphere was tense to say the least. Everybody had been aware of the smear campaign on the noticeboard. Now things had come to such a head that somebody was trying to get two players dismissed because of their beliefs. Comfort and Daniels were virtually on trial.

Graham Daniels took the lead and repeated the defence

they had made to Ryan. Whoever had made the complaint, he claimed, was telling lies that could cost them both a job.

'And,' concluded Daniels, 'I know who it is.'

'Who is it then?' demanded somebody.

All eyes were on the player responsible for the hate campaign but Daniels didn't look at him.

'I think you know who it is,' he said.

The player broke the silence. 'You Christians,' he spat. 'There are two of you. There'll be three tomorrow and then there'll be four. This is a football club not a church.'

It was as near to an admission of guilt as they were going to get. In the end Ryan dropped the matter and was big enough to offer Graham Daniels a new contract a few months later. Daniels has no criticisms of him. He remembers John Ryan as 'an honest man'. Earlier that year he had been open-minded enough to go and hear Billy Graham preach at Portman Road along with four or five other Cambridge players. Probably many managers in his situation would have acted the same way. Christians were a new breed in football at the time and no one knew quite what to expect of them. To John Ryan it must have seemed that a rare tropical disease was going around and his team had caught a double dose.

It was all a whirlwind for Alan Comfort. One minute he was an integral part of the team, the next he felt pushed to the very edge. The dressing-room had become a court room with God on trial and Comfort and Daniels as the key witnesses for the defence. How much of the tension at the club could be put down to the run of poor results is hard to say. Certainly no player could feel very relaxed when they knew they could be axed from the team next game. But the personal pressure on Alan Comfort had certainly increased since his decision to become a Christian.

'I didn't know much about the Christian faith,' he admits. 'But I knew it was impossible to just walk away from it.

In those early days I was thankful that Graham acted as a cushion, absorbing much of the tension. But there were times when I wished it all could have been easier.'

As far as his team-mates were concerned it must have been hard to fathom. When Comfort had arrived at Cambridge he was nineteen, single and full of his own success and earning power. He had stayed with some of the players in digs while waiting to buy a house. He had 'been out with the lads' and done all the usual things that players of that age do. At one stage he was even double dating two sisters with another player (naturally he didn't mention this to his girlfriend, Sue, back in Farnham). The Cambridge players knew Alan Comfort as 'one of the boys' – it was a big adjustment to accept him as a Christian who suddenly had very different standards about the way he lived. Not surprisingly they missed no opportunity to remind him of the things he used to do.

If his team-mates were cynical, Comfort soon discovered that his family and his girlfriend considered he had taken leave of his senses.

'For my own family it was a shock, a massive shock,' admits Comfort. 'They thought I'd joined a sect. That was their idea of what I'd done because in their eyes I'd suddenly become a fanatic, a lunatic.'

It isn't too hard to understand the reaction of his parents. Their son had left home for Cambridge as a promising footballer. Yet within a few months he was talking to them excitedly not about his career but about God and religion. They had done nothing to plant the seeds of such a change; someone else had to be to blame. They blamed Graham Daniels.

'I think they thought that Graham had influenced me, so they really disliked him. If he was in my house when my parents came to visit, they didn't like him being there. They made it plain a number of times that they couldn't forgive him. They saw him almost as a leader of a sect.

They understood it very much in that light. I wasn't going to a normal church because that meant you could just go to the Anglican church up the road and you didn't act the way we were acting.'

To be fair, Comfort probably didn't help matters himself. He was so excited about God that he talked with passion about his new faith whenever he saw his parents. 'In a way, if you could roll back the clock, I would do it all very differently,' he admits. 'I do feel that often my parents got the wrong end of it.'

His parents weren't the only ones to suffer. Alan had got engaged to Sue that year with the intention of getting married in the summer of 1985. They had been going out together for almost five years and must have felt they knew each other inside out. How could Sue have been prepared for her fiancé's sudden announcement that he'd become a Christian? From her point of view he began to change – and change quite dramatically. Alan also felt they were heading into unknown territory. His future wife didn't share beliefs that were now central to his whole life. It was not a promising basis for a marriage. After much soul searching he decided they would have to split up.

'It was my decision. She was very unhappy about it,' he recalls. 'But something had happened to me and she didn't understand it. She wasn't a part of it. My whole life was just starting to take off from a Christian point of view, and I needed space to try and work out what was going on. That was the hardest decision in the world because we really did love each other. There was no doubt about that. Whether it was an intense relationship or not, we did love each other. I think that in the months that followed, through to the summer, I did find myself questioning what I had done.'

Sue returned to her parents in Farnham and they stopped seeing each other. But the relationship was not over for good as Alan thought at the time. A chance meeting two years later was to mean a further twist in the tale for both.

Back in Cambridge another couple were saying their goodbyes. Cambridge United and John Ryan had never been a marriage made in heaven and this season their relationship had hit a particularly rocky patch. With relegation virtually assured by mid-February, Ryan paid the price of all football managers who fail to deliver. His departure from the Abbey Stadium also proved a fatal blow to the hopes of one of his players. Graham Daniels' form as a makeshift left back had persuaded Ryan that he was worth keeping in the squad. So Daniels was promised a new contract one week but the next he found that he was dealing with a new manager. Ken Shellito didn't take long to decide that the Welshman was surplus to requirements.

Graham Daniels' career had been in trouble from the moment Alan Comfort arrived at the club. He had suffered a long period in the reserves and then had a stay of execution under Ryan in the New Year. Shellito gave him a free transfer but he ended his career at the early age of twenty-four. During his final year in football he had been in increasing demand as a speaker at youth clubs and church events. With disarming honesty he admits that he discovered he was a better speaker than a footballer. Today he works as a pastor and evangelist for Christians in Sport, visiting the twenty or more Christian professionals in the football league and Premiership.

Daniels' departure meant Alan Comfort was on his own as a Christian at Cambridge. The two players have remained close friends to this day but their time at Cambridge together was not always easy. Like Alan's family the Cambridge players sometimes saw his conversion to Christianity as a copycat version of Graham Daniels. The jibes that he was Daniels' disciple were sometimes hard to take.

On the football field, Ken Shellito's arrival failed to stop the rot at the Abbey ground. His side lost the first four games under his management and Alan Comfort was one of the players dropped. The winger responded in two ways – by asking for a transfer and scoring a mesmerising goal for the reserves in a cup semi-final. The twenty-year-old winger took the ball from his own half, weaving past player after player before planting the ball in the back of the net. Even the referee stood and applauded. 'He must have run seventy yards and beaten half the Luton team,' said the official afterwards in a rare post-match tribute.

It was probably the most spectacular goal seen at the Abbey Stadium all season and reflects the two sides of Comfort's game at that early stage in his career. He was a classical winger capable of bringing a game to life and the crowd to its feet with a jinking run and cross down the touchline. Yet in the next game he could be a frustrating figure on the margins of the action. It is a criticism that has been made of far greater names such as John Barnes and Chris Waddle of England. Maybe it is something in the nature of wing play – it is the kind of inspiration that cannot be produced for ninety minutes twice a week. Old-fashioned wingers are loved by crowds but not always by managers who prefer a modern winger like Andy Sinton who covers the whole pitch and tackles back like a midfielder. The genius of the classic winger shows in flashes of brilliance which can change the whole course of a game. John Barnes' unforgettable goal against Brazil is a case in point: people ask, why didn't he do that every time he played for England? They might as well ask why all of Van Gogh's paintings are not masterpieces.

A winger is also only as good as the service he gets. Alan Comfort was playing in a struggling side which was usually on the defensive for most of a game. It is hard for any winger to thrive on a diet of long balls cleared upfield. The result was that Comfort never pro-duced the football he was capable of at Cambridge, and looks back on his first season as an up-and-down affair.

'I was like a yo-yo: one minute in the side and the next out. A losing side often sacrifices a winger first as a luxury they can't afford, but at Cambridge they just couldn't make their minds up. If the team lost I'd be dropped but if they lost the next match I'd suddenly return. I was in and out so much I didn't know if I was coming or going. A good manager knows that to get out of trouble you have to stick with what you believe is right. At Cambridge the management didn't have a clue what was right.'

No doubt there were other players whose form suffered as well as Alan Comfort's but it was his first season of league football. Looking back, he realises he still needed to serve a first-team apprenticeship. Even talented young players like Ryan Giggs at Manchester United were groomed for the first team over a period of time. 'You don't see them regularly until they're twenty, twenty-one,' Comfort points out. 'They've played fifty games already but they've never played them all together and they've learned their trade. There is a world of difference between careful grooming and being thrown in and out of a losing side from week to week'.

Comfort's transfer request was granted. Cambridge were hoping they would recoup the modest £15,000 they paid for him. But despite enquiries there were no firm offers that summer. The player's own comments in the local paper show that he was willing to leave the back door open to stay: 'I just wish I could have done more for the club. I hope things work out for Cambridge. Perhaps I will stay and be part of it. I will give 150 per cent if that happens'.

It was football-speak for 'I'm keeping my options open in case nobody signs me'. In the new season, Comfort came off the transfer list and was in the line up to face Hartlepool on the opening day of the fourth-division campaign. Cambridge won 4–2, but it was a false dawn.

Their poor run of form continued, and a few months into the season Ken Shellito followed John Ryan into the roll-call of ex-United managers.

His replacement in December 1985 was Chris Turner. Turner is a forceful character and a manager who succeeded in bringing the best out of Alan Comfort on the pitch – but off it they had a stormy relationship.

As a former centre-half, Turner had seen plenty of tricky wingers in his time. He soon decided that what Comfort needed was more guts and determination in his game. He made it his personal responsibility to give the young winger a rough ride in training. 'He spent all his time winding me up,' says Comfort. It wasn't an approach that you'd find in any FA coaching manual, but even the player himself admits that it got results. In Turner's first game in charge, Comfort scored a coolly taken goal at Torquay – and better displays followed. He began to recapture some of the confidence and form he had first shown on arrival at Cambridge.

But there was trouble brewing between manager and player. In the New Year of 1986, Turner became concerned about cutting the wage bill at Cambridge which left him with little room for buying new players. As one of the highest paid players at the club, Comfort was first into the manager's office. He was asked to take a cut in wages from the generous contract that Ryan had agreed to get him there. Comfort was reluctant to agree. Like any footballer, he was concerned to protect his future in a career that only lasts ten to fifteen years. He argued that it was unfair to ask him to take a wage-cut when other players weren't.

There were other things that bothered Turner besides money. During the course of a week he had Comfort in his office almost every afternoon after training. They would talk for half an hour – a long time in a manager's busy diary. Much of the talk was, surprisingly, about God. Comfort says he began to wonder where it was all leading.

'He asked questions that made out, at first, that he was interested in God. I was naive enough to think, "This guy's thinking about becoming a Christian. What an amazing thing to do!"'

Whether Turner's interest in Christianity was genuine or not, the discussions ended back down to earth with a bump in the hard world of professional football. Alan Comfort has never forgotten the day he was given his marching orders from a football club.

'Eventually he (Turner) said, "What I've got is this. I'm manager of a football club and I've got every player in this club totally committed to me. But you've got a day off for a college course that you have written into your contract." (Comfort was taking business studies at the time.) "Nobody else has got it. So I can't have you on those days. Also I can't be sure that you'll play for me on a Sunday, because you're a Christian. So what I've got is a team of totally committed people, then I've got you five days a week. I believe that the only way I'm going to be successful as a manager is if I've got people who are totally committed to me and this football club. You can't promise me that."

'I said, "I can. But why shouldn't I be able to have a day off to go to college? And I haven't said I won't play on a Sunday. We don't have games on a Sunday so why does anything need to happen on a Sunday?"

'He said, "It's the principle of total commitment. I'm going to ask you a question: when it comes to the crunch, is God more important to you than this football club and me?"

'I said, "Of course."

'That was the point when he said to me, "See that door? Once you've gone through it, don't come back."'

It was, as Turner said, a question of commitment. To a football manager, when a player signs for that club, it owns his total loyalty. If the manager asks you to play in a blizzard you do it; if he says you'll play better if you eat dog food before a game you eat dog food. This is not much of an exaggeration. Viv Anderson recalls how the great Brian Clough once ordered his players to take their tracksuit bottoms off and run through a field of stinging nettles.

'We were stung to high heaven but we all went: Shilton, Burns, Lloyd, Francis – all experienced internationals. So I wasn't going to argue about it. In fact we all had to go through again. It was the law of the playground but it worked because nobody argued back.'[1]

As Anderson implies, the law of the playground breaks down if one person refuses to join in. And the problem was that Alan Comfort no longer saw football as the ultimate authority in his life. When he had become a Christian, God had taken over the number-one place in his life. If it came to choosing loyalty between God and the Queen herself, there was no contest. It is a dilemma with a long history – the early Christians found themselves in a lion's den because they refused to accept Caesar as their god.

Some footballers, Gavin Peacock is one, seem to be able to manage their football career and their beliefs without the two coming into serious conflict. With Alan Comfort, God and football often seemed to be on a collision course. This time there appeared to be no way back.

Comfort remembers that he left the interview with Turner in a daze. 'In my football career I had never had a moment like that. I left. I didn't know where to go, what to do. It seemed absurd. I was confused. There's never been a point when I would have said that someone was more important than God from the moment I became a Christian.'

He returned home with his mind reeling with questions. He had just been told by his manager to walk out of the door and never come back. What exactly did it mean? Had Turner spoken in a fit of anger or did he mean what he said? Was Comfort's playing career at Cambridge over for good?

If so, who would employ a player who had virtually been told to 'get lost' by his manager?

For a brief unnerving period, Comfort felt he was in limbo. In the end, with the help of the player's union the PFA, the situation was resolved. But if he thought the whole affair had been a storm in a tea cup, he was soon to be proved wrong.

A few days later he received a telephone call from a friend, David Moyes, a former Cambridge player who was now at Bristol City. Moyes asked him a question that took him completely by surprise: did he know he was up for sale?

Although not unheard of in the game, it was the second time in his career that Alan Comfort had learnt about his future second hand. The first time he had read in a newspaper that he had signed for Cambrige. This time the same club were getting rid of him. When a player is put up for transfer a circular goes round every club in the football league to inform them of the player's availability. It is naturally common practice for the player himself to be informed before this happens. Comfort had received no such warning. He'd only found out because the manager at Bristol City, Terry Cooper, was interested in signing him and had mentioned the possibility to David Moyes. Cooper couldn't go through with the deal until the summer because he needed to sell another player to raise the cash to buy Comfort.

It was the only reassuring piece of news. At one point Chris Turner had warned Comfort that nobody would want to sign a Christian. The player had to face the possibility that his manager was right. One thing for sure, the Abbey ground wasn't going to be a comfortable place to be over the next few months.

He needn't have worried. Within a few weeks of the dispute he was called out of his Wednesday college class to receive a call from Chris Turner. As usual the message was brief and to the point. Turner had agreed terms with Leyton Orient. He wanted Comfort to go down for talks today and he didn't want him to come back.

Alan Comfort left his college and drove to London. On the journey he had plenty of time to reflect on the turn his life had taken. Less than two years earlier he had driven towards Cambridge on the same road as an excited teenager about to launch his career. He had started with ambitions of playing for QPR in the (old) first division, but since then his career had bumped along the bottom of the Football League. Now he was returning to London to hold talks with another fourth division side. It wasn't the rapid take-off to his career that he had anticipated. Still, he reasoned, he was only twenty-one. At least time was on his side. He was now a very different person from the quiet, naive teenager who had driven up the road to Cambridge. As a schoolboy he had only known success and praise as a player. With Cambridge he had seen the downside of football, playing in a relegation side in front of supporters who were used to losing as a way of life. Above all, he had discovered Christianity and his faith had been tested in the school of hard knocks. His whole career had been on the line more than once. What he needed now was a fresh start, a chance to recapture the form that had so impressed Tommy Docherty as a teenager and made him an England youth international. Maybe then his football career would start to take off. The question was whether Leyton Orient could provide the springboard he needed.

Notes

1. Andrew Longmore, *Viv Anderson* (Heinemann: London, 1988).

Chapter Seven

Caught in the Crossfire

It made a great back-page news story. Keith Peacock, manager of Gillingham, was sitting at the breakfast table thinking to himself that what his team really needed was a midfield player, one who could create chances for other players and score goals himself. But where could he find that kind of player?

'I had been trying to sign a midfield player for some time and had been quoted ridiculous amounts of money,' he remembers. 'One morning I looked up across the breakfast table at Gavin and thought, "Now there's someone who could do us a favour in midfield."'

There were other reasons behind Gavin Peacock's loan to Gillingham in 1987. He was approaching twenty and, two years after his league debut, was still fighting for a regular first-team place at QPR. Jim Smith had offered him a three-year contract, making it clear he wanted Peacock at Loftus Road. But he would stay as a squad player. As any professional knows, that's another way of saying you're a side dish to the main menu – squad players are in and out of the side if and when they're needed.

Peacock admits that patience isn't his greatest asset. In a profession where life ends in your early thirties, twenty is an age when footballers want to be out of the starting blocks and making ground. He was anxious to get on. When the chance of first-team football came with a month's loan to the third-division club, he grabbed it with both hands.

'At that time,' he says, 'I just felt I needed to play first-team football in midfield. My dad had that place at Gillingham and so I went down there and it was great. I really enjoyed it. I played well for them that month. When I came back I felt I wanted to go and they wanted to buy me. Jim Smith was good; he didn't stand in my way.'

It was Gavin's own decision but as usual he listened to his dad's advice. 'It was weird really,' he says, 'because he was the manager buying me and yet also the father advising me what the best career move was.'

For Peacock senior it was the first time that his ambitions as a manager and his role as a father could have come into collision. Looked at from the outside, some might say that Gavin Peacock was making a mistake leaving a first-division club to play for a team in the third. Alan Comfort, who made a similar decision to go to Cambridge United three years before, felt it was the biggest mistake he ever made. But Comfort and Peacock are very different players and personalities. Peacock was willing to take a gamble on himself that he could drop down a couple of divisions to return to the top level. He was leaving Rangers to prove a point.

'It is a hard way and you can really come a cropper because you play the odds against,' admits Keith Peacock. 'But Gavin felt confident enough to come out lower down and do what Steve Bruce did.' (Bruce also played for Gillingham in his early days before climbing to the highest level to collect a Premier League champions' medal with Manchester United.)

Keith felt there was no conflict in his advice as a father and as manager of Gillingham. The move would suit both sides. Gillingham would get a good player who could later be sold at a profit while Gavin Peacock himself would get the experience of first-team football playing in his preferred midfield position. Ultimately the gamble was to pay off. Gillingham later sold their midfielder for a club record fee of £250,000 and Peacock did eventually return to the top flight, albeit five years later. Who knows what would have happened if he had stayed with QPR? As it was, a shock was in store for both Gavin Peacock and his father. The normally quiet Kent club was about to be plunged into controversy.

With Gavin Peacock at Gillingham, the club were in a promising period of their modest history. Keith Peacock had been manager of the club for six years. In that time they had come close to promotion on so many occasions that it almost felt like they were trying to break an unwritten law that Gillingham belonged in the third division. In the last six seasons they had finished sixth, thirteenth, eighth, fourth, fifth and fifth again. If there was a title for the nearly men of football, Gillingham would have won it hands down. The 1986–7 season had introduced a new twist to the end of the season with the first introduction of the play-off system. Finishing in fifth place, Gillingham qualified along with Swindon, Wigan and Sunderland who were trying to avoid the drop from the first division. In the semi-finals Gillingham scraped past Sunderland after extra time to meet Swindon in the final. They beat Swindon 1–0 at home but lost 2–1 in the away leg. It meant a replay on neutral ground at Selhurst Park. As the fifty-first third-division match that season it broke a league record. Almost inevitably, Gillingham lost the game 2–0.

This was the history of glorious failure into which Gavin Peacock arrived in 1987. The expectation was that this was the season that Gillingham's fortunes must finally change. Such buoyant optimism can be found at every club at the

start of a new season, but Gillingham began as if they had
no more time to waste. Southend were crushed 8–1 and
Chesterfield annihilated by an astonishing ten goals. Even
Saint and Greavsie on television started to sit up and take
notice. Gavin Peacock was imported on 8 December to
add vision and first-division class to a side that was going
places until injuries disrupted their rhythm.

At the time Keith Peacock played down the father-son
connection, citing Brian Clough, Ken Brown and John
Bond as examples of other managers who had their own
flesh and blood on the playing staff. Yet the risks are
obvious. Other players are bound to be suspicious that
the son will get an easy ride. A father may be tempted
to give his son the benefit of the doubt when any other
manager would have no hesitation in dropping him. Also,
what happens if the son gets too familiar and talks back to
the manager?

The most famous example of the father-son partnership
in modern times was Brian Clough and son, Nigel, at
Nottingham Forest. Far from showing any undue favouritism, it often seemed that the outspoken Clough went out of
his way to be harder on his son than other players. Clough
junior was always referred to as the 'number nine' in public
– as if his dad had trouble recognising him without a football
shirt. It may have been a conscious decision on Clough's
part to show football superseded all family ties. He once
stated, 'If it meant getting three points on Saturday I would
shoot my grandmother. Not nastily, I would just hurt her.
That's how it gets to me.' It was perfectly in keeping with
Clough's contradictory nature that he also believed that
Nigel would have gained far more caps for England if
he hadn't been related to the loudest mouth in football.
It is a doubtful claim and probably says more about the
deep-down pride that Clough had in his son than about
the way England managers select their sides.

Keith Peacock was as proud as any father of his son,

but he also knew what was expected of him as manager of Gillingham Town. He must have realised that not every player at the club would welcome the news that the boss was spending £40,000 to buy his own son. Ian Docher, who was on the playing staff at the time, says that the dressing-room was split on the issue of Gavin Peacock's transfer.

'Half the players thought, "Ah well, this is it. He's going to be running the show, getting away with everything on and off the pitch." The other half were saying, "No, we've heard he's a good player. His dad will be fair and treat him like anyone else."

'I can honestly say that's what happened. It didn't take long for the split to come together because they appreciated Gavin's skill on the field. There were times when his dad quite rightly gave Gavin a good rollicking and he accepted that in the changing room. The players respected that on both sides.'

Gavin Peacock agrees that the relationship was never a problem. In fact he felt having his dad as manager positively benefited his game.

'I enjoyed it. He treated me just the same as any other player when we were at the club. In the game, if I was playing badly, he'd tell me in front of the others. If I needed a kick up the backside he'd give it to me. At the same time there was nobody that knew me better than my dad as a footballer and as a person. He knew how to motivate me and get the best out of me. So from my point of view it was great. And because he knew how to handle the situation there was never any jealousy or problems with other players.'

When pushed, Gavin will concede that it was a delicate situation which sometimes demanded treating him a little differently from other players.

'He wouldn't go overboard if I'd done something good. If I deserved a real pat on the back he might not say anything because if he did there might be a little bit of feeling that "it's just because he's his son". You've got to handle it the right way otherwise you can get jealousy from other players. But I got on well with the others there: they were a good set of lads at Gillingham.'

In football you have to earn respect. Players tend to judge a new team-mate first by what they see on the field, things like character and personality can wait until later. Ian Docher says that Peacock was well able to let his feet do the talking.

'I was the ball winning midfield player, Gavin was the ball player. I knew that once I won that ball I'd look up and I could give it to Gavin in any position, whether he was marked by one, two or three players, because I knew he was good enough. He was very fit and very dedicated. His dedication is second to none. He gave me confidence and, when I was going through a bad patch in my debut season in the first team, he would advise me. It's not often in your career that you get a chance to play alongside a top quality Premiership player.'

Everything should have been set for Gillingham, with their midfield bolstered by Peacock, to take the third division by storm and win the promotion that had proved so elusive.

Instead things started to go wrong. A number of key players got injured, and from 24 October to Christmas there was a run of poor results with only one win. The team dropped from promotion contenders to 13th place – the no man's land of mid-table. The season was only half over but everyone had expected Gillingham to be one of the pace-setters. The final straw came on 28 December when Aldershot handed out a 6–0 drubbing. The directors felt enough was enough. They gave Keith Peacock the sack.

Football throws up all kinds of ironies. In his last league game, the great Denis Law scored the goal for Manchester City that doomed his former club, Manchester United to the second division. Law said afterwards, 'After eleven years with United most of the people there were my friends and I certainly didn't want to put the nail in their coffin. I have seldom felt so depressed as I did that weekend.'

Keith Peacock might have echoed Law's last sentiments. His sacking was another of football's cruel ironies. He had been one of Gillingham's longest serving and most successful managers. At the start of the season he was hailed as a hero as his team crushed Southend and Chesterfield with scorelines more suited to rugby. Only three months later, a defeat of a similar kind saw him axed as manager. Even worse, his own son had only been at the club three weeks, bought at his decision and coming on his advice. The Peacock father-son partnership was probably the shortest in league history.

A short statement appeared in *The Times* report on 29 December 1987 from Roy Wood, chairman of the Gillingham Board of Directors. 'After carefully considering our recent results the Board have decided to relieve Keith Peacock of his duties forthwith.' It was the usual coded language designed to play down a situation which threatened to be explosive. The sacking unleashed a wave of angry protest among the normally placid Gillingham fans.

Gavin Peacock remembers hearing the news of his dad's dismissal with shock and disbelief.

'He called me into the office and told me that he'd got the sack. Then I had to go and sit in the dressing-room while he came in and told the players. They were all stunned and gutted. People were saying, "I can't believe it," because a lot of those players were in the team that had just missed out on promotion the year before. He'd done good things at Gillingham. Everyone was just stunned and of course nobody more so than the fans. It was a very emotional time.'

But even in life's worst setbacks there is room for

small moments of comedy. Ian Docher, who was only a
youth team player at the time of the sacking, recalls how
he heard the news:

'Keith came into the away changing room and told us
all to sit down. He said that the board had sacked him and
he'd be clearing his desk that day. Looking around the
changing room everyone was really shocked. Myself, I was
really upset because I had a great deal of respect for Keith.
But if you ask anyone, I'm a bit of a smiler. I remember
Keith looking at me right in the eyes as he said, "I've got
the sack," and I started smiling at him. In my heart I was
very upset and very angry with the board, but it looked as
if I was smiling and quite happy. I've known Keith a long
time now and it's a standing joke that he got the sack and
I started laughing.'

Many managers would have found little to smile about
at the time, but Peacock senior is adamant that he left the
club without bitterness.

'I'd always told my family, "One day I'll get the sack,"'
he says. 'I'd been six and a half years at Gillingham. We'd
been quite successful: half way in the league, won 10–0
and 8–1 earlier in the season. In any other walk of life
I'd have been ready for an extended contract and a good
increase in salary because managerially it had gone on a
very successful level. It doesn't work that way. On a whim
of a couple of results they say we're sacking this one.'

At the time only Brian Clough, John Lyall at West
Ham and Ken Brown at Norwich had served longer at
their clubs than Peacock. Brown went soon after. In the
modern football world only success is tolerated. Directors
are not interested in coming second or having an unlucky
season. They want silverware in the boardroom and fans
queuing at the turnstiles. Woe betide the manager who
doesn't deliver within two or three seasons of arriving.
Since there are ninety-two clubs in the league and Premiership, it follows that 90% are going to be disappointed every

season and the manager merry-go-round will continue. Even the greatest are not safe. Brian Clough steered modest second-division outfit Nottingham Forest to the league championship and two European Cup successes, but the first time his team were relegated, in 1993, he knew that his number was also up.

Keith Peacock's view is that you have to be philosophical to survive. 'It's difficult as a manager to stay at one place; you can't put in for a transfer. If you're going to be bitter about being sacked then you're going to end up as a very bitter person and at odds with the football world. You have to take it and look forward to whatever the next job is. In my time at Gillingham I was very happy. We were always in the top half of the table and the season before got to the play-offs. I left with the crowd saying, "Why has he gone? We want him back!" Maybe if I'd stayed for another two years they would have been baying for my blood.'

The word for the reaction of the Gillingham fans certainly wasn't philosophical. On 2 January 1988 the Kent club were entertaining Fulham. The home supporters used the occasion to stage a rowdy protest against Keith Peacock's sacking. What made matters worse for the board was that their former manager was spotted in the crowd. Keith Peacock maintains he was there like any other father to pursue his favourite hobby – watching his son play. 'It caused them a bit of a problem because the fans were chanting my name,' he shrugs. This is something of an understatement. During the match Gavin Peacock celebrated the New Year with his first goal for the club. After the final whistle there were scenes never seen before or since at Priestfield. Gillingham's ex-manager was leaving the ground when he was spotted by home fans. The crowd swept him up on their shoulders and carried him back into the ground. They took him to the directors' entrance and staged an angry demonstration. Banners were waved demanding 'Bring back Peacock' while the ritual chant of 'Sack the Board' echoed around the ground.

Needless to say, the Gillingham board didn't agree to either demand. Their response was to request that Keith Peacock stay away from home matches as 'a disruptive influence'. Chairman Wood also went on local radio to make a stinging attack on the fans.

The manager's job was given to Keith Peacock's former assistant, Paul Taylor, until the end of the season. Peacock senior soon received another job offer, ironically from his son's former team. He became reserve team manager for Queen's Park Rangers. The last laugh was at the expense of the Gillingham directors. Gillingham never recaptured the success they had had under their long-serving manager. They finished thirteenth (exactly the position when Peacock was sacked) and the following season sunk like a stone into the fourth division. Their former manager meanwhile went on to take charge of newly elected Maidstone United.

Where did all this leave Gavin Peacock? He had left a team riding high at the top of the football league to join his father at a third-division club. Within three weeks Keith Peacock had gone. Gavin was left two choices. He could demand a transfer or ride out the storm and play for the board who had sacked his dad. He elected to stay but it wasn't an easy decision. These days Gavin Peacock can talk calmly about that period in his career but there is no mistaking the note of contempt in his voice when he is asked about the Gillingham board.

'They were amateurs really. They didn't really understand the game. They panicked after one bad result and they fired one of the best managers they've had on record. He'd been there six and a half years and put them on the map. They were renowned as a good third-division side. All right, they weren't in the top three or four, but they were expecting that straight away. As we all know, teams

Top left: Gavin's early days. As mascot at his father's 1972 testimonial.
Top right: In the Newcastle kit.
Bottom: Training with his father in Florida 1980.

Gavin playing for QPR against Oxford during the 1987/88 season.

Gavin takes aim for Newcastle in 1992.
Pictures courtesy of Newcastle Evening Chronicle & Journal Limited

The proud father.
Gavin with Jake
(in Chelsea kit).
Hats courtesy of the
England youth team!

The one to watch.
Gavin at Chelsea.
Picture courtesy of Action Images

As a 17 year old, Alan is a guest player with Geoff Hurst, Martin Peters and Nobby Stiles, under the guidance of George Graham.

Alan jets off to his wedding after Orient's vital promotion winning game against Wrexham.
Picture courtesy of Sunday Express Newspaper

Honours from Leyton Orient where Alan was Player of the Year in 1985/86.
Picture courtesy of Phil Carpenter

Triumph! Alan celebrates his first goal for Middlesborough in September 1989.
Picture courtesy of Ted Ditchburn: North News and Pictures

Picture courtesy of Stuart Weir

Above: The Happy Couple. Alan and Gill.
Bottom: With Sarah.

come from the middle pack and make runs for promotion. It was only Christmas time when they panicked. It really didn't go down well with the players or the fans.

'I had the dilemma then whether I stayed or whether I left the club. I decided I'd stay because I'd come there to prove a point, and I wasn't playing for the directors as such – I was playing for my team-mates and myself, for my career.'

His father agreed. There was nothing to be gained by a show of anger.

'You could turn around and say you've sacked my father and so I'm off, or you could say I'll show you that my father made a good buy. I'll do what I have to do and develop as a player because that's why I came here. I don't have to be in love with the people who sacked my father but I can be polite and get on with the job.' He was well liked there, even by the board of directors. He was always polite but if they were complimentary he'd nod his head, he wasn't taken in by that.

Gavin Peacock played out that season at Gillingham and stayed for the next. It wasn't easy at first. For the players and the new man in charge he was a constant reminder of their former boss. The press too were not likely to leave a good story alone. They kept the controversy smouldering for weeks with questions to Gavin Peacock about his dad. Supporters of opposing teams were even less sympathetic. For a short while 'Your dad's got the bullet' became one of the favourite chants at Gillingham's away games.

It would have been an uncomfortable period for any player. Gavin Peacock was still only twenty years of age and making his way in football. It says a lot for his character and determination that he rode out the storm and gained the respect of those around him.

Ian Docher was among those who were impressed.

'A lot of other players would have cracked or gone down,' he thinks. 'As you can imagine he was very upset, but the way he conducted himself on and off the field – with the press asking him questions and the reactions he got from away supporters – was brilliant. That could have got to a player but he had that self-control, that inner ability to stand firm. It opened my eyes and made me respect him as a person.'

Docher got to know Peacock better than most. Not only did he play alongside him in midfield the following season, but he had started to take an interest in another member of the Peacock family – Gavin's younger sister. Lauren was caught up in the soccer world from as early as she could remember. When her dad took over at Gillingham, Lauren was often at the ground on a match day helping to make the half-time tea. She stopped going when Keith got the sack but Ian Docher kept asking after her.

Eventually Gavin got the hint and arranged a double date at a pub-restaurant with himself and Amanda as the other couple. The evening was a success and Ian Docher started to go out with Lauren. He spent a lot of time at the Peacock household. It is one of those houses where the phone and doorbell are in competition for attention. Keith Peacock occasionally announces he is going down to Piccadilly Circus to read the paper in peace and quiet.

Docher had heard rumours about Gavin Peacock's religious beliefs. Like many players, his reaction was a mixture of scepticism and curiosity. In the mornings he would sometimes get a lift into training with his team-mate. The journeys were broken by Gavin playing his collection of Christian music tapes. 'I would join in the songs with him,' says Docher. 'Whatever he tells you, Gavin is one of the worst singers I've ever heard besides myself. But we'd have a good old sing-song – then I would start to listen to the words, listen to what they meant. And as I was singing them, in my mind I'd be thinking, "This makes sense." Gavin never pushed his faith on me but he'd always answer my questions in a way that made sense.'

By this point Peacock was becoming known as one of the rare breed of Christians in football. At Queen's Park Rangers he had still been adjusting to his new faith. He felt no need to make a dressing-room announcement of his conversion like Alan Comfort. Peacock's approach from the first has been to let other players come to him. This isn't so much a conscious decision, he says, as a question of personal style.

'I think I know how I would feel if someone was pushing something at me. Especially with footballers, you would get them to put a block up immediately. You can't do it. Maybe some people have got a talent for it but I don't think it's the right way to do it. If you talk about Jehovah's Witnesses for example, people say, "Oh no, not them!" They put their foot in the door. It just turns people off. I think if you live as an example of your faith, people know that you are a Christian and maybe they'll come to you and say, "What is it about?"

'There will be times I suppose when you have an opportunity to say something, but I've always found it better if someone asks me. I don't feel awkward about telling them because then I know they want to hear. I feel that is my role – to be a Christian footballer.'

The rule is the same one that Daniels and Comfort followed at Cambridge. On one occasion it was a policy that may have saved their jobs.

Peacock is a different character to Daniels and Comfort. The former Cambridge team-mates both have something of the evangelists' fire. Both are natural speakers who would enthusiastically seize any chance to talk in public or in private about their faith. Peacock will talk openly to anyone who wants to know, but he denies that he is cut out for a speaker or an evangelist. He sees his role mainly as an example – to show it is possible to be both a footballer and a Christian in what is often seen as a hard, macho sport.

He has not had to go looking for opportunities to speak of his faith. At every club since QPR, his reputation has gone before him. Early on at Gillingham, TV South approached him to do an interview about his beliefs. The piece was shown on the regional news the day before a game. Peacock admits he was nervous about the reaction he would get in the dressing-room the next day. As it happened, only one player made a comment: 'I saw that piece you did on TV. It was really good.'

Peacock plays down the problems of being a Christian in the male club which is the football world, but there were awkward moments at Gillingham. Ian Docher tells one story which illustrates how Peacock's faith sometimes meant that he chose to stand apart from others.

On long away journeys up the motorway to the less glamorous corners of the league – places such as Wigan and Carlisle – players would get bored. To pass the time they would bring videos to watch. According to Docher, *Indiana Jones* or *Back to the Future* were not on the menu. The videos were more likely to be hard-core porn.

As soon as the video was loaded and switched on, a chorus of jokes would be directed at one player. Gavin Peacock was on his way to the back of the coach. He would go down the steps to the door which led to the luggage compartment under the coach. Once inside, he would climb into a sleeping bag and remain there for an hour or two. Regular as clockwork, when the tape had finished and the coach was nearing the away ground, Peacock would appear again, greeted by another chorus of ribald comments.

Docher remembers, 'The players used to speculate: did he go down to get some sleep or did he go to stop the temptation, because once he watched he might have wanted to continue?'

It is just one example of the way Peacock knows he will be watched by other players as a committed Christian.

A football club is a hothouse atmosphere where players spend five days a week in close proximity. Hours on the training ground, travelling on coaches and sharing hotel rooms mean that any private hobbies or unusual interests will soon come to light. Anyone who is different will find themselves the butt of jokes. Peacock often says that if you turn up in a new tie at a football club, players will give you stick for it.

As a Christian, Peacock is an easy target. During five-a-side games, players will sometimes appeal to him for an 'honest decision' when there is a dispute over a ball having crossed the line. If Peacock rules in favour of his own side he is greeted with howls of disbelief, 'Call yourself a Christian?' Other players are allowed to gain a few yards during sprint races in training, but if Gavin Peacock does it then his 'cheating' will be seized on with mock disgust.

Peacock accepts this sort of treatment cheerfully. If it is his turn to be the butt of jokes one day, it will be another player the next. He also knows that the same players who have a laugh at his expense may want to know more about his beliefs in private. In the long run he hopes that he may have some effect. 'I've never had anyone become a Christian at a football club through me but I've had a lot of players ask me about it and become interested. And you never know that down the line they may become Christians and you may have played a small part in that.'

Ian Docher would certainly credit Peacock as a strong influence. In their time at Gillingham together he watched how Peacock dealt with the pressure of his dad's sacking and envied his sense of contentment. In hotel rooms Docher would switch on the TV while Peacock read the Bible he carried with him. This led to questions about Christianity. For Docher it was the start of a two-year search which ended with him becoming a Christian himself. Eventually he was put in touch with Graham Daniels, the Christians in Sport evangelist, but it was Gavin Peacock, he says, who first started him on the road to faith.

Gillingham ended the 1987–8 season well short of the promotion place they had expected to fill. Peacock meanwhile was proving that his father had made a bargain buy. He scored the goal of the season in a 2–2 draw at Brentford, winning back possession before bending a twenty-five yard shot around the keeper. 'I took a leaf out of Kenny Dalglish's book,' grinned the twenty year old afterwards. 'I saw him score a goal from a similar position against Arsenal a few years ago.' Other comparisons were made of Gillingham's Young Player of the Year. Radio 2's Pat Murphy singled him out on 'Sports Report'. 'Built like Maradona only not as good with his hands,' joked Murphy.

In the following 1988–9 season, Peacock was the only bright spot for Gillingham fans as their team were relegated. He played in forty-four games and scored nine goals, fulfilling the promise he had shown as an England under-nineteen international.

'Gavin was head and shoulders above the rest of us,' recalls Ian Docher. 'He was playing better and better every game. The crowd loved him. I think he'd be in every Gillingham supporter's favourite team.'

It wasn't enough to save the Kent club. After having come so close to the second division, they sank into the fourth. Gavin Peacock's plan to leave first-division QPR and work his way back to the top seemed to have backfired. For the moment he was on his way down rather than up.

Alan Comfort meanwhile was travelling in the opposite direction. It was not long before the two players would find themselves squaring up to each other on the football field.

Chapter Eight

The Flying Winger

From the moment Alan Comfort met the Orient manager, Frank Clark, he knew things would be different.

The deal was signed quickly at a bargain price of £10,000 which probably reflected Chris Turner's decision to cut his losses and offload the winger. Newspaper reports of the transfer only hint at the gulf that had opened up between player and manager. What mattered for Alan Comfort was that the unhappy Cambridge chapter of his career was brought to a close.

'Frank Clark,' says Comfort, 'is the gentleman of football – and did I need a man like him after my experience at Cambridge. When I arrived at Leyton Orient I was told that he would speak to me and I found him a very sincere and honest man. For the first time I felt I might well have somebody there who at least I could trust as a manager.'

Orient were lying just behind the promotion pack when Comfort arrived, and it was clear that Clark felt the former Cambridge player could be the tonic his side needed. In a team of 'bargains and free transfers', Clark today describes Comfort as 'one of the best buys I ever made at the club'.

Things took off. From the moment he arrived, Comfort

started to rediscover the form that had made him an England youth player. Clark played an attacking formation with two out-and-out wingers – young Lee Harvey on the right and Comfort on the left. Between them they gave many fourth-division defences an afternoon they'd want to forget. Orient missed out on promotion that season but Comfort had grounds for optimism. He had rediscovered his goal touch and his confidence. In the top-of-the-table clash with Stockport he scored the winner and turned in what one paper called 'a superb exhibition of old fashioned wing-play'.

'We had a much better team and all I needed was a good team,' he says. 'Cambridge was just desperate. I'm not a tackler, a "backs-against-the-wall" player. I'm a player that you have in the side when you've got good players around you and then I can really go. At Leyton Orient they had enough good players; they just needed someone to beat defenders and cross the ball into the area – that was perfect for me.'

Statistics bear him out. At Cambridge he scored three goals in eighty games. During his three years at Orient he scored forty-seven goals in one hundred and fifty games. An average of one goal every three games is a strike rate many centre forwards would envy.

At last it looked as if his career was on the up but, paradoxically, as a Christian he was struggling. It wasn't that he had doubts; it was a question of trusting God for certain important things. A future wife was one. His split with Sue had left a gap which no one since had filled. Oddly enough, for a twenty-one year old in a profession not short on glamour, Alan Comfort felt lonely.

'Not lonely because I couldn't meet any girls – that was far from the truth. But lonely because I didn't meet girls of my own age who had the same enthusiasm for God. My faith had changed me. It excited and drove me. But the girls I met could never understand this, and it was hardly their fault.'

As a Christian he believed that God knew what was best for him, but as a person he was naturally impatient. He wanted something to happen today, not tomorrow. Back in Cambridge he had moved to a new church to try to meet people nearer his age, but in that city 'they were all doing degrees'.

'I wanted to meet people who wouldn't talk about politics or something,' he says. 'It was all very pretentious and there was I a professional footballer.'

With his team-mates he felt much more at ease. They shared the same world: the pressures and risks of riding the weekly switchback that is professional football. Church felt too much like a middle-class Sunday outing where he didn't fit in.

The result of this build-up of frustration and loneliness was a crisis of faith during a summer holiday. Alan went to Corfu with an old school friend and decided he would have 'two weeks off' from Christianity. It was a desperate gesture of rebellion and not a totally happy experience.

'I was outrageous for two weeks,' he remembers. 'I've never been so sick. My friend couldn't believe it. Over two weeks I drank as much as I could and attempted to meet as many young girls as possible. But then at the crucial moment I would bottle out of going any further. It was as if I could rebel up to a certain point but then I would automatically stop. I desperately wanted to forget God, but I just couldn't.

'Each morning I'd get up and sit on the balcony with my Bible shut on my lap. I couldn't open it. I was so ashamed. Yet I didn't know what to do. I was caught in the middle. I wanted my friends and I couldn't do without them anymore.'

Maybe his conversion to Christianity had happened so fast that a time of questioning was inevitable. But it

wasn't that Alan Comfort had any real doubts about
God's existence; it was more that inside he was crying
for help – he had reached breaking point.

Returning from the holiday, he steered well clear of
any Christians out of a sense of shame. Graham Daniels
he especially avoided, but it was his former Cambridge
team-mate who eventually tracked him down. Daniels
listened to the saga of the holiday. He assured Alan
Comfort that, whatever his failures, God loved him more
than enough to forgive him. 'I was desperately sorry,' says
Comfort, 'and I felt the struggle lift from me when I asked
God to forgive me.' Looking back on it today, he believes
the crisis was about more than a lack of relationships; it
was a question of whether he would completely and utterly
trust God for every detail of his life.

The storm had passed and something new emerged from
the wreckage. The crisis had marked an important turning
point in Alan Comfort's life. He returned for pre-season
training at Brisbane Road in July 1986 feeling a different
person. 'Good holiday?' the other Orient players asked
him. If only they had known the answer.

He had decided he would trust God for everything,
including a life partner. That meant an end to looking
in every bar, disco and even church. Instead he would
depend only on prayer. At the time, Comfort was reading
a book by the Korean pastor, Paul Yonghi Cho, who leads
what is probably the biggest church in the world. Cho
suggests an approach to praying for a husband or wife
that is direct to say the least. He advises you to write
down ten things you want in a partner, then pray over
the list every day. According to Cho, if you get it right,
God will then answer.

Comfort smiles at the memory of drawing up his list
today.

'I get very embarrassed about those prayers because it
sounds so immature. In the real world not all our prayers

appear to be answered, or not in the way we expect. But maybe it wasn't so naive.

'The first thing I wrote was that she must be a Christian, somebody who would be as enthusiastic about God as I am. I found myself saying things that I'd never said before: I said dark hair instead of blonde because I'd always gone out with blonde girls and I thought she had to be different.' (The person he eventually married has dark hair, so perhaps Cho knows a thing or two.)

Eighteen months later his prayer was to be answered in the most dramatic and unexpected way. Yet the following year it seemed as if life was about to come full circle. Comfort was into his second season with Orient and driving home to see his parents in Aldershot. As he approached the town centre he saw a woman get out of her car and walk up the high street. It was Sue.

Two years had passed since they had last seen each other, and in that time Alan had never really got over her. He pulled into the car park where he had seen her and turned off the engine. His mind was still racing. Should he try and catch her up or would it be a big mistake?

He walked to the bottom of Aldershot High Street and struck a bargain with God. If he met Sue before he reached the top of the road then he would take it as a sign that it was meant to be. He had passed three shops when a woman came out of Marks and Spencers and walked straight into him. It was Sue.

Alan remembers that the conversation got off to an astounding start.

'The first thing she said to me was, "I've become a Christian." I couldn't believe it. We went and had a cup of coffee. It felt so incredible that after all that time somebody would say that they'd become a Christian. She seemed very genuine about that.'

Soon they were going out again as a couple and it was as if they had never been apart. They were seen in church together on Sundays. On one occasion, when Alan was the guest speaker, Sue was introduced as his fiancée. It had never been settled in so many words, but from that point they agreed they would get married. There was no reason to delay and the date was set for six months' time.

It was after the Christmas of 1987 that things started to go wrong again. Alan can still picture vividly the time and place where the painful conversation took place. Life's important scenes are not always played out in dramatic surroundings and this one took place in a Guildford Pizza Hut.

'We were sitting waiting for our pizza when she dropped the bombshell. Sue told me that she still wanted to marry me but she had lost interest in God and church. I was stunned. I thought the whole Christian thing must have been a facade; you don't just "drop" God. I felt so stupid. After letting go and trusting God over a long period of time, I felt I was trapped again. If only you could just switch emotions on and off. If I could have said, "Sorry Sue, that means we're finished," it might have been easier. But I couldn't.'

The weeks that followed were an agony of indecision. Three years before he had dumped Sue, but this time it was different. They'd come so far. How could he go back on the commitment he'd made to her? Yet if they went ahead, did their marriage have any real chance?

At the time, Comfort was living with his parents in Aldershot and commuting to London daily by train. He would sit staring out of the window in a daze as the future flashed before him with painful clarity.

'I knew what it would all mean. It meant going to church on my own. Having her friends and my friends arguing over whether our children should go to church or not. Even more important, it meant that I couldn't share what made me tick as a person. When I spoke at a church the excitement would end with me. If somebody became a Christian the moment wouldn't be shared. And it would make it impossible for me ever to work full time in Christian ministry. I saw so many dreams disappearing.'

Sue's conversion to Christianity had seemed to put the last brick in place for their future together. But now the whole house was in danger of crumbling. Again, Alan turned for help to his closest friend, Graham Daniels. They spent a weekend talking and praying over the situation. Despite the painful dilemma he was facing, Alan says that God gave him hope by showing him three things. The first was something from the past that resurfaced. Graham told him that he believed God had gifted him to be a preacher. It was a prospect that still scared the wits out of Alan. In any case, how could he go down that route if his wife didn't share his faith? That was the second thing. Before the weekend was over, Graham confided to Alan that he felt the engagement with Sue was over. It wasn't advice or a voice from God, just a clear impression. But on arriving back in Farnham hours later, Sue confirmed that the engagement was off.

The anguish involved in a broken engagement can only be understood by those who have been through it. Alan Comfort had twice come close to marrying the girl he loved and twice seen it all fall to pieces. By rights he should have been sunk in the depths of misery. Instead what he felt was a mixture of relief and excitement about the future.

'Of course I was sad, but it was also very strange that inside I felt I had just been set free. People would say to me, "Let your emotions go. Cry and let it all out." But I didn't want to cry; I wanted to shout at the top of my voice that God is alive in me and he is taking care of my life.'

There had been three things from the weekend and it was the last that explained his sense of excited anticipation. Several different Christians had been praying for Alan, and three told him separately that in the very near future he would meet the girl God wanted him to marry. He was realistic enough to know they could be wrong. What they were passing on was something they felt God saying as they prayed. Alan didn't have to wait long to find out. Only six weeks later he met the girl he believed was the answer to God's promise.

The story begins with Gerald Williams, the BBC tennis commentator, who knew Comfort through Christians in Sport. On one Sunday, Williams invited the footballer to go to a service at a large church in Guildford. Alan had spoken there once before on the occasion that Sue had been introduced as his fiancée.

He returned that Sunday and sat down on his own, expecting to meet Gerald Williams later. There was a girl singing a solo on the platform at the front of the church. Alan recalls first seeing Jill vividly:

'As I sat there I felt in my mind that God said to me, "This is the girl that you're going to marry." I said to God, "If this is right, then you're going to have to turn on every green light there is. First because I don't know how I'm going to meet her, and secondly because I can't afford to get it wrong again."

'I didn't walk up to her and say, "God has told me we're going to get married." Instead I prayed that first we'd meet. It was all very embarrassing in a way. As she was singing I nudged the guy sitting next to me and said, "She's all right, isn't she?" Then, when the service ended, she walked off the stage and came straight towards me. Suddenly I was petrified. My legs were shaking and I said to God, "You didn't have to answer this quick!"

'I got up but she walked straight past me to the guy I had nudged during the service. They hugged each other. How embarrassing! I thought it must be her boyfriend.'

As it turned out this wasn't the case. Comfort was just thinking he must have made a big mistake when Gerald Williams walked up and introduced Jill. Her first words to Alan were, 'Where is your fiancée?' Not the easiest of questions to answer to a girl you're hoping to marry.

Jill remembers her first sight of Alan in less complimentary terms.

'When you're singing,' she says, 'you always know when somebody's eye-balling you. I could see that this person was eye-balling me so I avoided his eyes. Afterwards we were introduced and we got on very well. We were invited back to coffee at Gerald Williams'. There was another chap there at the same time and it was quite funny because Alan and he were both trying to work out who was going to get me there and who was going to take me home afterwards.'

Alan has Gerald Williams to thank for getting ahead of his rival. He succeeded in walking Jill home afterwards and asked if she would go out with him again. The answer wasn't exactly overwhelming. Jill looked in her diary and offered him a date ten days away. She was attracted to Alan but far from being impressed at the prospect of dating a professional footballer.

'I really liked him,' she remembers. 'We chatted nonstop and we laughed a lot. But I was nervous because I knew he was a footballer. It's not exactly a "done" profession to be seen associating with – lawyers, solicitors, doctors, anything like that was fine. But footballers are a bit more "iffy". It was mainly because I knew what other people's reactions would be. It didn't come between me and him at all. I didn't worry, but I knew other people would worry about me being seen with a footballer just because of the impression people have of football.'

Many girls might have thought Alan's career glamorous but Jill didn't come from the sort of background that saw career goals as the ones you put in the back of the net. The reactions of 'other people' she was nervous about included her own family. They lived in Northern Ireland

and were mainly professionals in medicine or law. As Jill explains:

'In Northern Ireland, football's not at a high point of professionalism and isn't played to any great standard. People don't play football as their profession; it might be something they do for their town. It's not like football is in England at all. There's a totally different concept about football. To say you were going out with a footballer was really a nothing.'

As a 'nothing' Alan Comfort's chances of marrying the girl he had just met seemed slim. But he was so convinced of what God had promised that he determined he would tell his family. If it all fell into place it would naturally be useless to tell them after the event that God had planned the whole thing. He had to speak out now when it all seemed so impossible.

The very next day over tea he informed his mother and sister, Donna, that he'd met the girl God wanted him to marry. His mother's response was a model of maternal wisdom: 'Well, can you leave making your mind up until you've at least gone out with her once?'

Jill and Alan went out on their first date. There was a second and then a third. On that occasion at Jill's house (she was a social worker living in work accommodation) the couple prayed together. Alan recalls, 'We both looked up at each other and I said to her, "You know, don't you?" She said, "What are we going to do?"'

After only three weeks there was an unspoken understanding that they were talking about marriage. Alan says that Jill had also known this from the moment they'd met and was 'scared to death'. Her fear was that her family would never accept that she was going to marry a professional footballer.

A date was set for a visit to her family in Northern Ireland. As the day drew near Alan became increasingly nervous. Jill's father was a farmer, her mother a teacher, and the rest of the family was bulging with professionals in law, medicine or the clergy. The children had been sent to public school and brought up as God-fearing Irish Protestants. All of this was out of Alan Comfort's experience. Jill's other boyfriends had been surgeons and accountants. Yet here was he, a nobody footballer in their eyes, expecting the family to accept him as their future son-in-law. Things might not have been so bad if he'd been able to adopt a shrug-of-the-shoulders attitude to their reaction, but everything depended on it. The couple had agreed that if at the end of the fortnight Jill's family did not accept Alan, then they would call the whole thing off. If God meant them to get married then he would have to find a way to overcome all obstacles. For a couple hopelessly in love it was a courageous step of faith. The question was, would it work?

Alan relates an incident in the days leading up to the trip that reveals the funny side of the class gap he was confronting.

'Jill was worried about my eating habits because I didn't squash my peas down on my fork and apparently you're supposed to squash your peas down. We went to a restaurant and Jill said, "Order the peas." Seriously, I learnt how to squash them on the back of my fork that evening. She felt that if it was embarrassing to the family then that would be the end of me.'

The week of the ordeal finally arrived. Jill's mum and dad received Alan politely and said nothing to criticise him. But the undercurrents were not promising. Alan remained quietly in the background for the first week and it was clear that the family didn't take him seriously as part of Jill's future. When football was mentioned at the dinner table, most of the conversation centred around hooliganism, which was rife at the time.

'I spent five or six days when I felt ashamed,' recalls Alan, 'because I'd moved into a different world and they

just didn't understand or accept my job. That's what I was.
I couldn't help hooliganism and I wasn't a hooligan, but
it almost felt as if I was a part of that. It was obviously
really hard to deal with and I didn't feel as if I had any
real chance.

'I believed that God had said to me that this was the
girl I was going to marry and I could see it was all going
down the pan. It was a horrible feeling because you had
got no control. Jill still loved me. I still loved her. But
if her parents didn't change, we were finished. We sat up
night after night praying that God would somehow change
the situation.'

On the Sunday morning, Alan and Jill attended her
family's Baptist church. After the service, the minister
approached Alan and asked if he would like to speak
that evening. Not a sermon, just fifteen minutes to tell his
own story. For Alan it was like being handed the chance
to take a decisive penalty in the last minute of a cup final.
Although he'd often spoken in churches before, it had
never been in such crucial circumstances. If he stood up
in front of everyone and made a fool of himself, he might
as well get on the next plane home. So far he had failed
to make any impact; this was his last chance. Everything
hung on those fifteen minutes. Either God would use them
to turn the situation around or what he said would bring
the roof down on him.

The evening came and the moment in the service when
Alan was introduced. He stood up with the eyes of the
whole church – and Jill's family – on him. He began to
speak of how he had become a Christian and his early
days in football. He told of a time at Cambridge when
he had been dropped from the side. An elder at church
had heard the news and gleefully took him on one side.
'You see,' he said, 'now God is calling you out of football.'
At the time Alan had wondered, 'Why is my job such an
embarrassment? Can't God work in footballers too?'

When he finished speaking, he dared to glance over at Jill's mother. Her reaction was critical to all his hopes. She had clearly been moved and later cried when she was alone with Jill. It was the turning point they had hoped and prayed for so desperately. Following the service, Jill's mother invited all her friends back to the house to introduce them to her daughter's new boyfriend. Once she admitted she'd been wrong about Alan she lost no time in making amends.

Alan didn't let the grass grow under his feet either. During the remaining week he went to Jill's father and asked for permission to marry Jill. Jill's father gave his consent on the condition that the couple agreed to wait a year. Later in the week he slipped into his daughter's bedroom early one morning and stood at the foot of her bed. 'Jill, are you happy?' he asked. 'Yes,' answered his mystified daughter. It wasn't until Alan proposed to her on the plane home that she realised why her father had asked the question.

There was only one sad note. During the whole fortnight Alan Comfort didn't have the chance to show that he could eat peas correctly.

Jill and Alan got engaged in 1988 and set their wedding for 3 June the following year. They were careful to check with the football league that all fixtures would be over by then, including the play-offs. In any case, it didn't look as if Leyton Orient were likely to have much interest in such things.

The 1988–9 season had started disastrously with the O's taking six games to record their first league win. Some pride was restored with an 8–0 thrashing of Colchester but at Christmas, the watershed of the season, Orient were only lying in mid-table. In February the league announced new dates to extend the season – the play-off final would be on . . . 3 June. Still, Comfort wasn't worried – there was little chance that Orient would be in that game unless they performed a miracle in the final run into the season.

What happened was just that. The East London club put together a run of form that sent them soaring up the table – and the player most responsible was Alan Comfort himself. Together with Kevin Campbell, a talented teenager on loan from Arsenal, Comfort tormented defences to end the season with nineteen goals. The newspaper headlines from February onwards tell the tale:

ORIENT REVEL IN TWIN COMFORT
Leyton Orient 3 – Burnley 0

Alan Comfort rocketed Leyton Orient back into the promotion frame with a wonder strike on Saturday. He cut inside to unleash a glorious twenty-five yard drive that angled its way into the top corner. In a sensational second half, Comfort was everywhere. He scored twice and wreaked havoc on a shell-shocked Burnley defence.

COMFORT IS THE KEY TO PROMOTION
Hereford 1 – Leyton Orient 1

Orient winger Alan Comfort just can't stop scoring goals. Every time he scores the Os don't lose and that's a record that managing director Frank Clark hopes will last for the rest of the season. Clark said: 'He could play a vital role in the final stages. But he's only doing what he is capable of. Every time he gets the ball around the edge of the box he is lethal.'

EASTER FEAST
Leyton Orient 4 – Hartlepool 3

Orient hauled themselves back into the play-off zone on Thursday night with this thrilling win against struggling Hartlepool. Many more games like this and manager Frank Clark will need a new set of finger nails.

COMFORT-ABLE RIDE FROM THE VERY START
Leyton Orient 3 – Rochdale 0
When Alan Comfort struck a 12th minute opener Rochdale may as well have packed up and gone home. For when Comfort scores this season, Orient don't lose.

Lincoln 0 – Leyton Orient 1
The 1–0 win clinched Orient's place in the top seven and now the scene is set for the nerve-racking finale.

For Comfort, the play-offs had extra reason to be nerve-racking. In the final run-in he had scored twelve goals in a burst of form that brought him to the notice of many bigger clubs. But by doing so he had also landed himself with a seemingly insoluble problem. The wedding invitations had been sent out; guests had booked flights and hotels; it was too late to change the date. The only way out he could see was to miss the vital last game if Orient got to the play-off final. It was a heart-breaking decision to have to make.

Orient met Scarborough in the play-off semi-finals. Comfort, with his mind on his wedding problems, didn't play well but the team scraped through 2–1 on aggregate. They were into the final and the clash with Saturday 3 June was a reality. There was only ten days to find a way out.

The first thing they did was to contact one of Alan's sisters who was married to an editor at the *Daily Mirror*. He sprung into action to find a newspaper that would print the story and help solve the problem. The *Sunday Express* agreed to print it and promised they would make their helicopter available on the day. It was a start, but still left plenty of unsolved problems. The wedding was set for three o'clock in Bangor, County Down – precisely the same time as the match kicked off. Even if the wedding was put back to 5.30 p.m., Comfort knew he had no chance of getting there in time.

He outlined the situation to his manager, Frank Clark. Clark knew that Comfort was vital to his plans. 'We actually developed a way of playing that season to get the best out of Alan,' he recalls. 'Instead of playing with two wide players, we played a midfield player wide on the right and we gave Alan the licence to come in field and play among the front two. It meant that he sometimes got into positions in front of goal where the ball would just drop at his feet. And in those areas he was lethal with either foot.'

Clark knew that Comfort could be the difference between the two sides on the day and was prepared to do almost anything to make sure he played. In the end what he did was to pull an amazing sting on everyone involved.

'I had to con everyone including the football league, the police and Wrexham into thinking that twelve o'clock was the ideal time for us to kick off rather than three. It had a precedent in that most of the games we'd played on Sunday had kicked off at twelve and had always gone off peacefully and trouble free. I don't know how I managed to persuade everybody that it was the right thing to do. Our local police preferred it but Wrexham didn't like the early start for their fans. I made no mention of the wedding in Ireland.'

A game involving twenty-two players and coaching staff, 13,000 fans and local police was ultimately rearranged to suit one man's wedding plans. If the football league had known they might not have seen the funny side.

It was still going to be tight. The plan was that the helicopter would take Alan straight from the match to the runway at Heathrow Airport where he would board a British Midland plane to Belfast. Jill's uncle, a surgeon, got in touch with a British Midland pilot he had operated on and got him to arrange for the shuttle to be delayed at Heathrow until Alan arrived. From there, the *Express* proposed hiring another helicopter to the wedding. If everything went according to plan they would touch down in Northern Ireland with just enough time to make it to the wedding.

A week before the wedding, Jill returned to her parents' home still with misgivings that her bridegroom was going to make it to the church on time. The *Express* had not counted on the fact that nobody can fly a plane or helicopter over Belfast without weeks of security checks from the police. With two days to go, this fact came to light. The army stepped in with an offer of taking Alan in a Lynx helicopter. That meant him sitting with his legs hanging out of the open side door. Alan has a fear of heights and knew he couldn't do it. Time was running out. The day before the wedding a flight was finally found to take Alan from Aldergrove Airport to Newtownards – a short distance from Bangor and the wedding.

Everything was arranged, but the timing was planned like a military operation; there was no room for anything to go wrong.

On the Friday night the wedding rehearsal took place at the church without the bridegroom. 'There was only me, my bridesmaid and my mum and dad,' says Jill. 'There wasn't another soul there. And it brought it all home that tomorrow was very much up in the air – we didn't know what was really going to happen. That was horrible. An awful lot of tension everywhere.'

On the day, Jill sat in her parents' house listening to the game on the radio along with her relatives and other wedding guests. Among them was Gerald Williams, the BBC sports commentator. Jill remembers: 'He kept running to the phone saying, "This is Gerald Williams from the Beeb. What is happening there? We need to know."

The news from Brisbane Road was bad. It seemed half of East London had turned out to see Orient try to win promotion. There were so many supporters trying to get

in that the kick off really did have to be put back for
safety reasons. Comfort sat in the dressing-room knowing
that every ten minutes that was lost meant his wedding
deadline was tighter.

The game finally kicked off twenty minutes late. It
went well at first for Orient. They were 1–0 up until early
in the second half when Wrexham equalised. The game
drifted towards the last ten minutes. Extra time loomed
– a disaster for Comfort's plans. He was aware of the
Sunday Express helicopter circling the pitch overhead.
With eight minutes to go, Lee Harvey crossed from the
left and three Wrexham defenders stood rooted to the spot
as Mark Cooper lashed in Orient's winner. The crowd of
13,355 erupted and no one was more relieved than Alan
Comfort. The last five minutes of the game he spent near
the touchline, keeping as close to the players' tunnel as
possible. After a frantic finale in which Wrexham almost
grabbed an equaliser, the referee put his whistle to his
lips and blew. Orient had won promotion and the fans
and players began the biggest Eastend knees-up that
Brisbane Road had seen for years. But Comfort didn't
have time for celebrations. When he heard the final
whistle it was like the starting gun for the first leg of
his 400 mile race against time. He sprinted off the pitch,
had a quick shower and grabbed a bottle of champagne
and his wedding presents from his team-mates (mostly
unprintable gifts for his wedding night). Then he fought
his way through the crowds to reach the field at Hackney
marshes where the helicopter had been forced to land by
the crowds.

The helicopter took him to Heathrow and landed on
the runway where the 3.30 p.m. British Midland flight to
Belfast had been delayed on his behalf. At this point a
farcical element crept in as Alan relates:

'As I got off the helicopter, I went to try and shut the
door and the pilot shut the door from inside. He crunched

my thumb in the door and took half of the end of it off. It wasn't as if I needed to go to hospital but I'd lost half of the flesh part of my thumb and it was just pouring with blood. The pilot left and I stood there thinking, "I can't believe this!" So I got onto the aeroplane with blood pouring out of one hand and a bottle of champagne in the other. I suppose I looked like a typical footballer. I kept telling people, "I'm going to get married but we won." I was in a state of exhaustion after the game.'

The British Midland flight touched down at Aldergrove Airport and Alan climbed aboard the four-seater private plane which would take him to Newtownards for the final leg of his journey. Once on Irish soil a telephone call told the wedding party in Bangor that the groom was on his way; they could start to get ready. For Jill that was the moment when she knew her wedding day was on and the tension of the build-up began to ebb away. The day had begun dull and drizzly but as the bridal party came out onto the lawn to take photographs the sun broke through. There was another sign from the heavens as a plane flew overhead; inside was a relieved Alan Comfort, just a few minutes behind schedule.

Alan was met at Newtownards by a member of the church who happened to be the chief of traffic police. That meant they could break the speed limit on the twenty-five minute drive to Bangor. The groom finally arrived at the house – sweating profusely and blood dripping from his thumb – to be met by the TV news cameras from Ulster. Even then the farce wasn't over. Alan takes up the end of the story.

'They said to me, "We've run you a bath. Get yourself ready." I'm thinking, "How do I get my suit on? I've got to get my clothes off and suit on without pouring blood everywhere." They said to me, "We've put hot water in. All you've got to do is put in cold. So I go up to the bathroom and their cistern packed up. You couldn't flush

the toilet and you couldn't work the cold tap. Graham
(Daniels) was there. He had only arrived that day and
he was my best man. We both looked at each other and
I knew I needed to try. So I put hot water all over myself
to try and get ready to put on my morning suit. My thumb
was bandaged up with a handkerchief.

'We went straight to the church. We arrived and we were
just a bit late. The church was packed – it had probably
been packed for an hour. As we were getting married,
the blood was dripping on the floor because my thumb
was going berserk at the time. I was trying to explain to
Jill. She suddenly saw it and realised there was all this
blood. Sweat was dripping off me too. It was one of those
situations you can't really believe. The pastor of the church
came up and said to me, "Look I know you haven't got a
clue what we're going to do, but just say what I tell you
to say."'

There was one final ordeal left. They had asked Andrew
Wingfield Digby, chaplain to the England cricket team
and Director of Christians in Sport, to preach the sermon.
Wingfield Digby took them at their word and preached
for nearly forty minutes. The bride and groom were
left standing throughout. Alan, having been up since
7 a.m., played a vital game and travelled 400 miles while
constantly losing blood from his thumb, cannot tell how
he didn't pass out. Looking back on the day, despite the
bizarre incidents, Alan Comfort says it was a moment he
would return to again and again.

'When the game ended I knew that not only was I going
to get married, but it meant quite a big move in my football
career. So it was one of those days that brought a whole lot
of things together; not only all those things that I believed
God had said, but also my career suddenly took off. I know
I was exhausted but I could sit back at the end of the day
and see that for me it was a point where everything I could
ever want, and more, I'd got.'

Moments of such perfect happiness are rare in life. Perhaps if Alan Comfort had known what lay down the road in less than six months' time he would have been less impatient to know where his future lay.

Chapter Nine

When the Saints

For a player whose ambition is to play at the highest level
in league football, Bournemouth is an unlikely stepping
stone. The sedate English resort nestling on the south
coast is a place where you might still get a good audience
tucked into their deckchairs around the bandstand on a
Sunday afternoon. Out of season Bournemouth is sleepy.
In the height of summer it opens one eye and receives
the invasion of tourists with the air of a duchess forced
to open her ancestral home.

Portsmouth, Southampton, Brighton, Bournemouth –
the south coast can talk nostalgically of Pompey's glory
days after the war, but in modern times there has been
little to rival the footballing dominance of London and
the north. In 1989 the manager with the unenviable task of
trying to drag Bournemouth towards the impossible dream
of first-division football was Harry Redknapp. As a player
with West Ham, Redknapp had plied his trade among the
finest in the league. To Bournemouth the second division
was still a novelty: when they were promoted in 1987 it
was the first time in their history they had been beyond
the third division.

On slender means, Redknapp had managed to recruit

Luther Blissett, the former Watford and England striker. Blissett was in the twilight of his career but still capable of the scorching pace and explosive finishing that had taken the (old) first division by storm in 1983 when Watford had finished runners-up to Liverpool. Blissett could provide a finish but Redknapp knew his side still lacked bite in midfield. He had already seen the player he wanted to replace Ian Bishop, who had just left Dean Court for Manchester City. When Gavin Peacock became available at Gillingham in the summer of 1989, Redknapp paid a club record fee of a quarter of a million pounds. It was a big fee for a twenty-one year old, but Redknapp was investing in a star of the future.

'Gavin has got tremendous potential,' he said at the time. 'I am not looking for him to be another Ian Bishop. The boy is a fine talent in his own right and everyone will see that for themselves.'

As far as Peacock was concerned Bournemouth represented the chance of one step up the ladder that led back to the (old) first division. He was joining a side respected for playing good football and managed by an old friend of his father's. Keith Peacock went with him to sign the deal.

At one point it looked as if Alan Comfort would join the Cherries alongside his old friend, but in the end Bournemouth could not find the cash for both players. Comfort headed north while his friend made the move to the south coast.

There were other changes on the horizon. In February 1989 Gavin had got engaged to Amanda with the intention of waiting a year to get married. With the move to Bournemouth the couple were faced with the options of living together or waiting out a long separation. As Christians the first was against their principles and the second held little appeal. They decided instead to bring the wedding forward to September. That meant it would have to be fitted in around the football season.

The wedding was fixed for a Sunday. The day before, Peacock played a home game against Blackburn and celebrated by scoring his first goal for Bournemouth. Then he drove back to south-east London for his stag night. The wedding was held in Barneshurst at the church where the couple had both become Christians. Then it was on to another football ground – this time for the reception. Keith Peacock had recently become manager of Maidstone United, newly promoted to the football league and playing at Dartford football ground. The reception was held in the social club there.

As they drove away in the car decked out with the obligatory tin cans and 'Just married' sign, Gavin and Amanda knew there was no blissful long honeymoon ahead of them. They had their honeymoon night in a hotel just off the M3 at Basingstoke – chosen because it was half way on the road back to Bournemouth. In the morning, Amanda had to drive the bridegroom into training – he didn't even get a day off work!

It was not the most romantic start to a marriage. A footballer's life for ten months of the year revolves around training and playing matches. Marriage to a player means a strange and unpredictable life which has its drawbacks. Amanda admits she found the adjustment to the new routine hard at first.

'You can't take a weekend away. You can't go out on a Friday or a Saturday night. All holiday has to be taken between mid-May and mid-July. There's no Easter or Christmas break. But I'm pretty adaptable. I like the life because it's very exciting, never monotonous, there's always something happening.' She is quick to point out that although football takes her husband away at weekends and on pre-season trips abroad, she sees more of him than most couples.

At Bournemouth Amanda endeavoured to further her football education by attending home games. Even today she happily admits she is no fan of her husband's profession.

'I'm not interested in football, only Gavin's games. I'll watch home and away games whenever I can. With Gavin coming from a footballing family, even his sister Lauren knows a lot more about football than I ever will. I think he likes it that way – it gives him a bit of a break. His mum, his dad, his sister and grandparents all know about football. He talks to me about his game but I can't really comment because I don't know anything about it. There's nothing worse than an ignorant person pontificating on something they know nothing about!'

Amanda was one of only two partners who attended Bournemouth home games. Some clubs are very keen to encourage wives and families to come to matches – Newcastle even ran a creche on Saturdays – but there was no players' lounge at the south-coast club to encourage socialising.

It can be an odd experience to sit in a crowd of several thousand people who all feel they have some ownership of your husband. Gavin's mother, Leslie, who has probably seen him play more than anyone, admits:

'Sometimes it's hard as a wife, even as a mother, to sit in the stands and hear the comments from the odd bods, and to just sit there and say nothing. You feel like putting them straight. So many of them talk so much rubbish. I've sat there before now and heard people behind me telling others what good friends they are of Keith Peacock and his wife, how they've been to our home. They've given all this spiel, and you feel like turning round and saying "I am this person you're talking about and I've never seen you in my life." But you can't get involved. You just have to sit there and take the good with the bad.'

Amanda's reaction during a game is to divorce her

husband in her mind from Gavin Peacock the footballer and fans' idol. Although she will watch his matches, she doesn't associate the player out on the field with the same person who will come home at the end of the day.

'Some wives shout at the games, jump up and get really into it. But I sit very quiet,' she says. 'The only time I get worried is when he goes down with an injury. Sometimes those tackles can be the end of your career. You hear of players swallowing their tongues and that's my worst nightmare. I can imagine myself running down the gangway to try and reach him.'

Another occupational hazard is that a player has little control over his future. Where many people have the luxury of planning to stay in one job for several years while they buy a home and put down roots, the footballer never knows where he'll end up from one season to the next. A transfer can mean an upheaval for a player's family to a completely unknown part of the country – Peacock has played in London, Kent, Dorset, Tyneside and London again in the space of eight years. A transfer may prove the make or break of a player's career. Each move has to be weighed carefully and Peacock says his faith plays an important part in every decision.

'I've always prayed about different moves, particularly the Bournemouth and Newcastle ones. I've never had a "word from God" on it, but I've put it into his hands and said, "If you don't want me to go then I know you'll tell me in some way." When I've gone to the clubs I've had a good feeling that it was the right thing to do.'

It is not merely a case of rubber stamping. On one occasion Peacock made a decision that could have back-fired disastrously. When playing for Newcastle in the first division, he had the chance to join rivals Middlesbrough in the Premiership. Commonsense would have said that a bird in the hand was worth any number of magpies in the bush, but Peacock turned down the move. His reasons centre on a visit to Ayresome Park and a pact he made with God.

'It was just a feeling I got about the place. It's a nice club, not as glamorous as Newcastle, but Middlesbrough were in the Premiership. Newcastle were in the first and we didn't know how we were going to do. I turned down the chance of the Premiership and turned down a chance to postpone the decision as well. I had freedom of contract; I didn't have to sign for Newcastle then, but I'd set a deadline. I'd said to God, "If you want me to go somewhere, make it happen before this date. I'm going to make a decision on the options I've got then." I felt I should do that. And I turned down the chance of the Premiership playing against the Manchester Uniteds and Arsenals.'

In contrast, Newcastle kicked off their season against humble Southend, but started an unbeaten run that eventually saw them romp away with the first-division title. Middlesbrough meanwhile were relegated. Peacock made the right decision; the rest is history.

Back in 1989, Bournemouth's most expensive acquisition was beginning to be in demand as a spokesman for Christianity in football. The TV South report at Gillingham was followed by a similar programme at Bournemouth which highlighted Peacock's faith. Letters had begun to arrive too, asking him to speak at a church, youth club or public meeting. As his career has taken off he has found himself more in the public eye and the letters have increased from a trickle to a steady flow. Gavin Peacock admits that he has to turn most of them down. For one thing, there is not enough time to satisfy the volume of requests that he gets. As a professional his first commitment is to his club: it would be inexcusable to play badly on a Saturday because he had travelled a long distance to speak the night before. Peacock's week is a disciplined routine where training, diet and rest are

all organised around match days. On only one occasion
has he ever agreed to speak the day before a game.

He is also well aware that fame can be exploited by
others. Each letter is read and considered carefully on its
merits:

'You can tell a lot of the time if they want to get you
along just as a name to bring in a few extra people. I've
had letters saying, "Come to our church to be the star
attraction." I'd be put up on a pedestal and it wouldn't be
followed up by anything. Whereas others would go along,
tell my story, and there might be some follow-up from
it for anyone who wants to know more.'

Again, Peacock doesn't see himself as a speaker in
the same mould as Graham Daniels, the evangelist for
Christians in Sport. Peacock is willing to tell his own story
to football fans or the media but he maintains that his first
role is to be an ambassador for the Christian faith within
the professional football world. This is perhaps less easy
than it sounds, for on and off the field, there are plenty
of pitfalls for a player who tries to live by moral standards
that many consider outdated in the nineties.

Watch any professional football match on a Saturday and
words like honesty, fairness and sportsmanship are not
the first that spring to mind. Modern football is big business. When Maradona's 'hand of God' ejected England
from the quarter finals of the 1986 World Cup, it probably cost English football untold millions in the spin-offs
a nation gets from winning the world's greatest trophy. Every Englishman bridles at the reminder of the
Argentinian's 'cheating' in winning the game, yet ask
how many English footballers would have admitted to
handball in Maradona's place and you would probably
get few takers. By and large footballers would blame the
referee for not spotting the offence. They are out to win
the game and if they can get away with a push or a dive
then the referee should take the blame.

Even Bryan Robson, the former England captain widely
admired as a model professional, has admitted he would
commit a 'professional foul' if it would prevent a goal: 'If
someone went through and I could catch him by bringing
him down, I'd bring him down. If I didn't, I'd feel I'd let
my team-mates and my fans down.'[1] He goes on to say
he would never kick a player when the referee's back was
turned – but the professional foul is different, not only
legitimate but a responsibility to your team. Nowadays
FIFA has ruled that a player should be automatically
sent off for fouling a player who is through on goal. Yet
the professional foul can still pay off as Ronald Koeman
showed against David Platt in the World Cup qualifier in
Rotterdam in 1993. Koeman not only got away without
a penalty or a sending off for his cynical tackle on Platt,
he scored a few minutes later to send England out of the
World Cup.

Gavin Peacock, in contrast, feels there are things that he
won't do, even if it meant the difference between winning
and losing a game.

'I wouldn't try and con a referee by diving for a penalty
or something like that. I try and play an honest game,
that's all I can say. Honest by the rules and honest to
myself, the manager and the team by giving 100% even
if I'm having a bad time out there.

'People say it's a physical sport – and it does demand
your aggression. You've got to have that aggression to do
well in it. But I would never go out to injure an opponent
or deliberately try to put them out of the game. I'll go in
for a tackle. I'm not renowned as a ball-winning player,
but I'll go in for tackles and I'll be aggressive in the way
I play the game. I'll try not to react if I'm getting fouled
or bad treatment. Fans say that they've noticed that.'

It isn't always easy. Team-mates will tell you that
Peacock has a temper which he has to keep in check.
He is not naturally cast in the mould of, say, Gary

Lineker who used to climb back on his feet after each crude tackle with the air of a born martyr. There have been occasions where giving 100% has led to flashpoints on the pitch. On one occasion Peacock was booked for squaring up to a player whose scything tackle had just sent him into orbit.

'I do react now and again,' he admits. 'It's a very emotional game. You're at ninety miles an hour out there. Things happen and your temper can get the better of you sometimes.

'I think sometimes that if you say you're a Christian people think that you're supposed to be holy and perfect, but as Christians what we're saying is we're not perfect. You're still going to swear now and again. You're trying not to and you don't swear as much as you used to, but sometimes your temper will get the better of you. Sometimes you will worry about things that you know you shouldn't do – heat of the moment stuff. It is something that I will obviously work on and probably will always be working on. We'll never be perfect but God's definitely helped me there.'

To back up his claim he points to a disciplinary record of only four or five bookings in eight seasons. Even then, two of the bookings he claims were for mistaken offences. Twice, as a Newcastle player, he threw the ball back to a player for a throw in and the player let it run. The referee, thinking the ball was thrown in temper, booked him for ungentlemanly conduct. Maybe sportsmanship has become so rare these days that referees find it hard to recognise.

In American sport there is a saying, 'A tie is like kissing your sister.' Winning is everything. Managers often wax lyrical about players who are 'hungry' for success. They are the kind you want in your side – players who will sweat blood to win and be devastated if they lose. Footballers often say they are 'gutted' in defeat. It may be a cliché, but it effectively conveys the feeling that losing is like having the heart ripped out of you.

There is an apparent problem here for a sportsman like Gavin Peacock who is a committed Christian. There are plenty of other famous Christians in sport: Kriss Akabusi in athletics, Bernhard Langer in golf, Glenn Hoddle and Cyrille Regis in soccer are just a few. Yet the doubt is often expressed – are they hungry enough to be winners? Does the belief that they claim gives them an inner peace also take away their killer instinct?

In the football world, Graham Daniels has a story which nicely sums up the dilemma.

'When I had just become a Christian and was still playing professional football, we were doing an exercise at the end of training. The players each in turn took a shot at goal. If you scored you were finished, if you missed you had to do it again until you scored. Everyone was pushing in to get to the front of the queue and I was keeping out of it. After a bit the coach said, "Blodwyn, you haven't had a shot for a long time. What's up?" I replied "Just waiting my turn, boss." He sneered back, "Blessed are the meek!"[2]

Today Daniels would say he was wrong not to stand up for himself. There is no room for being a doormat in sport. Gavin Peacock similarly denies that his faith has blunted his will to win. He is often cited as an example of dedication and commitment to younger players. Kevin Keegan has said of him, 'If there's a more professional and gifted player I'd like to meet him.' Peacock is single minded in the way he approaches every game, making sure he is at peak performance level. If anything, Gavin Peacock claims that his faith has made him a better footballer.

'The fact that God is central to my life has not made my football worse at all. It's only made it better to a certain extent because I've been able to relax more in my football. I just carry my faith through it,' he argues.

'I know what managers are thinking: that if you see football as everything to you then that's your lifeline and if it goes wrong, that's it. Whereas a Christian believes that God's got it all in hand. But I think that you have your job and God has something he wants you to do in life. He wants you to do it to the best of your ability and to work at it 100%. The best of my ability is the best I can offer anyway as a footballer.'

As an attacking midfielder who has also played up front, Peacock knows he is expected to score goals. 'Hungry' is a word that again comes to mind in describing the great goalscorers like Law, Greaves and Lineker. They had an almost insatiable hunger for goals. Terry Venables once said of Lineker that if you took a photo of any goalmouth incident around the six-yard box you would find him somewhere in the picture. Peacock does not presume to be in Lineker's class, but nevertheless recognises something of the same goalscorer's instinct in himself.

'I have this sort of hunger to score goals in training and in games. As a goalscorer you've got to want to. If you score one, to score two; if you score two, to get three. It's that little bit of single-mindedness about the goal.'

Keegan once said after a game that if Peacock scores twice he wants to take even the goal kicks to try and get his hat-trick.

Are goalscorers born or made? In Gavin Peacock's case, his father says the instinct had to be cultivated as a boy:

'He had an eye to score goals but I had a real passion to score goals. He was quite happy to make them. I tried to tell him that goals are very important. At the end of the day, all the highlights people see on TV are the goals. People ask, who scored the goals? That's the end product. Once he got the taste of being a goalscorer then it took off. You do get that thirst for it, whether it's a two-yard shot or a twenty-yard bullet.'

Today what is notable about many of Peacock's goals is his courage and determination to score. There is a typical photo of him scoring a flying header in a first-division game against Brentford. At the moment of the ball crossing the line, the studs of a defender's boot are only an inch from his face.

Peacock is one of life's natural competitors. No doubt it is another part of his father's character that has rubbed off on him. Like most young boys, Gavin competed against his father in games from an early age but, unlike other children, his dad didn't let him win. Keith Peacock decided on this rule after an incident at a holiday camp when Gavin was seven.

'We used to pretend to have boxing matches and he always used to knock me out. One year we went to a holiday camp. There was a boxing competition and he thought, "I'll go in for that." On the day they were moving in pairs down the front. Gavin was next to this frail little feller, a bit smaller than him. And the little feller was looking at Gavin and just ran away. So another boy was moved down who was two years older than Gavin, fractionally taller but physically he had more about him. Gavin wasn't fazed – he went into the ring and put his arms on the ropes like a boxer. I'd heard from someone else that the other boy had done a bit of boxing. Gavin hadn't, other than box me, but he thought, "If I can knock my dad out, well . . .". He was given a thumping. But all credit to him, he hung on there and recovered himself and got by. So after that I thought, when you come to beat me you'll have to beat me on merit.'

The father-son competitions are still going on today in the Peacock household. There is no quarter given whether the game is head-tennis or tiddley winks.

'I'm very competitive with my dad,' admits Gavin with

may occasionally accompany them to a nightclub. But they know that after a glass of wine or a lager he is on the Perrier and will probably be one of the first off to bed. It is not just his principles as a Christian that are at stake, his background has taught him that family life is important. His idea of a good time is to spend an evening with his wife, Amanda, and young son, Jake.

'Some players on away trips are out nightclubbing with the lads all the time. But Gavin's never done that,' says Amanda. 'We've always felt that we got married to be together, not to go out with friends here, there and everywhere without each other.'

Peacock is conscious that as a professional footballer he is an example for thousands of football-mad schoolkids. He accepts that all footballers are role models to some extent.

'Look at Gazza – the way he wears his hair, the clothes he wears. Youngsters copy him. When Hoddle was a role model in his Tottenham days he used to wear his shirt outside his shorts. He was one of the first ones to do it, but then all the kids started doing that. They're copying their heroes aren't they? If you're playing for Tottenham it's to a large extent. If you're playing for Gillingham, in that area the kids are looking to their heroes in the Gillingham team. You see it with kids in Sunday football. The goalies will start shouting like goalies on the telly. They don't know what they're saying but they've seen their heroes on TV.'

Few would claim that professionals have a good record in this area. The craze in schoolboy football for spitting on the pitch, kicking the ball away at free kicks and arguing with the referee can all be traced back to the antics of the Saturday men. Peacock hopes he can offer an example of a different kind. When he was at Newcastle, a mother wrote to him about the influence he'd had on her son.

'Her son had seen an article in the programme about

me being a Christian. He'd been a gambler – into fruit machines and that kind of thing. When they'd been away on holiday he'd taken £2,000 for his addiction. Since he'd read the bit in the programme he'd started going to church. The family were Christians themselves. A little spark like that is encouraging.'

Playing for Bournemouth the adulation of the Geordie faithful at St James's Park must have seemed like another world. Peacock played there for the first time on a cold windy night in February 1990. Bournemouth were lying comfortably placed, tenth in the (old) second division. The game was to be a turning point for both Peacock and his club. Newcastle won comfortably that night 3–0 and Bournemouth began a steady slide down the table.

On the stairs after the game, Peacock stood with a team-mate, Sean Brookes, and surveyed the huge stadium which had echoed to the chants of the Tyneside faithful during the game. 'What a club this must be to play for,' they both agreed. From that night Bournemouth must have felt that the fates had moved to live in the north of England. After having occupied a permanent place in the top ten they slid toward the relegation zone at an alarming rate. The squad was decimated by injuries – Peacock claims the hospitals were kept busy with something like seven operations on Bournemouth players that year. Harry Redknapp had no money available to buy replacements. Survival or relegation hinged on the final match of the season. As chance had it, the game was at home to Leeds United who needed to win to secure the second-division championship. Bournemouth also needed a win, but even if they lost, Newcastle could throw them a lifeline by beating Middlesbrough. Against all expectation Newcastle lost, Leeds beat Bournemouth and, to add injury to insult, the Leeds fans invaded the seaside resort and wrecked the town. In one of the worst examples of planned football hooliganism in recent years, the away fans wore T shirts proclaiming 'Leeds invasion of Bournemouth 1990'.

For Gavin Peacock the season had ended on a sour note. Unbelievably he had suffered relegation with a club for the second season running. He had just put a deposit down on a house in the Bournemouth area but knew his ambition to play at the highest level could not afford a drop back down to the former third division.

Alan Comfort was also facing hard questions about his future. He had joined Middlesbrough at the beginning of the 1989–90 season. His friendship with Gavin Peacock was renewed when the two players met on opposing sides in the early part of the season. In the game itself, Comfort's side came out on top. Blissett scored a spectacular goal to put Bournemouth ahead but on the stroke of half time Comfort worked his magic on the left and his raking cross was powered home for the equaliser by Bernie Slaven. Middlesbrough got a second after half time to run out 2–1 winners. Bournemouth's man of the match, as on many occasions that year, was Gavin Peacock.

Matches between the two sides had a remarkable record. On the three times the Cherries had previously played at Ayresome Park. Boro had won and gone on to celebrate a promotion party at the end of the season. On this occasion it was to be relegation which was more on the minds of both sides. After the game, Comfort and Peacock got together to catch up on old times. They had kept tabs on each other's fortunes since their QPR days and had met several times at Christians in Sport dinners. Little did they know that later that year they were to become near neighbours in the northeast. Gavin Peacock, who had stood on the steps of St James's Park in February, was about to see the dream of playing in that stadium come true. The opposite was true for Alan Comfort – his dreams were about to be shattered.

Notes

1. Quoted in David Hemery, *Sporting Excellence: A Study of Sport's High Achievers* (Collins Willow, 1986).
2. Quoted in Stuart Weir, *More Than Champions* (Marshall Pickering).

Chapter Ten

Shattered Dreams

The day he got married, Alan Comfort had placed himself in the best shop-window available. When the play-off finals take place at the end of the season there are only two or three games taking place in the whole country. Almost every club manager is watching their TV set. Comfort was out of contract at Orient and knew that his nineteen goals had attracted attention. Before the honeymoon was over he was phoning his agent to find out which clubs had thrown their hat into the ring.

The honeymoon was luxurious: a ten-day Caribbean Cruise followed by a week-long stay in America. But every honeymoon has its disaster story – in Alan Comfort's case the disaster was nearly his last.

'We flew into Miami and we were catching an internal flight to Florida,' he remembers. 'There was a delay – we waited for six or seven hours. Eventually it got to the last flight of the day and they decided to put a plane on.

'As soon as we got up in the air we looked out and suddenly there was this mass of cloud. Jill and I just looked at each other. It was a tornado. The plane lost control in the air and went everywhere. People were screaming, people were thrown out of their seats. We didn't see any cabin crew – nobody could move. We were all over the place for a time which seemed like eternity – I would actually say possibly fifteen to twenty minutes. We wondered whether we were going to die. We just held onto each other. An awful thing went through my mind. "God, I've waited three years to get married and you do this to me. Couldn't you have left it another week?"

'The news the next day was that a plane had gone down and 133 people had died. It was tornado season. They don't put the planes up. We were on the edge of it – we weren't in it because we wouldn't have survived. Everybody thought we were going to die: you know when your moment has come. Jill took three days to recover she was that shocked.'

On their return their honeymoon tales made them the ideal couple to invite for dinner parties. They brought their flight forward to return three days early. It was partly because they didn't like Miami ('We thought you were going to get killed every time we moved') and partly because Comfort had learnt from his agent that several clubs wanted to buy him. The newly weds were anxious to know where they were going to live.

Several clubs had been impressed by Leyton Orient's goalscoring left winger, among them Bournemouth, Bradford City and Middlesbrough. All were in the old second division and Comfort held talks with Bournemouth first. He actually shook hands on a deal with manager Harry Redknapp but things fell through. The reason was that Bournemouth paid a club record fee for Gavin Peacock instead. Comfort and Peacock both knew of the Dorset club's interest and as old friends had talked enthusiastically about the prospect over the phone.

'In some ways we were really looking forward to it because it would have been nice to play for the same side,' says Comfort. 'We both felt that putting the two of us together at a place where we would have had high profile as the new signings could have had a real impact.

'In professional football, as a Christian, you're making a stand all the time and nobody outside football really understands what you're doing. There are times when you think, "Did I do the right thing? Was I too jumpy, too sensitive?" If you've got somebody else with you, you've got a chance to help each other try to find the right balance. But it wasn't to be. When it came to the crunch they were trying to get both of us on the cheap and they just didn't have the money to buy both players.'

Instead Alan Comfort took the long drive up the A1 to the north-east and Middlesbrough. Peacock was to follow the same route a year later. In some ways the two players' careers have run on parallel tracks from their QPR days, both proving their ability in the lower divisions before making their name with big clubs in the north-east.

Middlesbrough were a club with both passion and pride. In their heyday during the 1970s they had won what was then the second division with a record margin of fifteen points (and this was in the days of only two points for a win). They had occupied their place proudly in the first division for seven seasons until the beginning of the eighties saw them relegated. With the formidable combination of the ex-Derby pair, Bruce Rioch and Colin Todd, in charge there were high hopes that Boro could return to the top level.

Alan Comfort knew it was the club for him as soon as he set foot inside Ayresome Park.

'I remember standing on the pitch thinking, "I'm going to be playing here soon." Most people just have ordinary jobs; you don't often get very close to your dreams. I was.'

Ayresome Park was the promised land at the end of a long road for Comfort. From his schooldays he was destined for professional football but he had never imagined settling for the lower divisions. His aim had always been to play for a big club in front of a big crowd. Tommy Docherty had singled him out at fourteen. The England youth selectors had confirmed he belonged to the cream of the young players in the country. Clubs from Manchester United to QPR had queued up for his signature. Then had come the move to Cambridge United at nineteen, the loss of confidence and the years in the wilderness of third- and fourth-division football. Some players are happy to play out their careers in the lower divisions, knowing they have reached their level. But Comfort was different. He always felt that, given the chance, he could perform on a bigger stage. In a few weeks his dream was about to become reality.

Middlesbrough may not be among the aristocrats of league football, but they had upper-class aspirations. They are one of those clubs that seem to have a longstanding visitors' pass to the Premiership – never a permanent resident but always likely to be back again soon. They had a ground with a capacity of 30,000 and the club commanded loyal and passionate support in the town. When Comfort arrived he was surprised to find people recognised his face. They would greet him in the paper shop with a nod and a hearty 'Welcome to Middlesbrough'. Ayresome Park is as much at the heart of Teeside as shipbuilding once was.

Boro had just fallen from their latest spell in the top flight but were convinced they had the squad to make a swift return. Comfort from Orient and Trevor Putney from Norwich had been recruited to a side that already included £2 million-rated Gary Pallister, Bernie Slaven, Stuart Ripley and Peter Davenport. Comfort spent much of the pre-season sitting in the stands watching Ripley, an England under-twenty-one international, play on the left flank. It wasn't until the final countdown to the season that he got in the side. When the team was named for the opening game against Wolves, Alan Comfort was so unprepared that he had to borrow a pair of boots from another player.

'For the two days before the game I just couldn't sleep,' he recalls. 'It was so exciting and I was nervous. You suddenly reach that point where everything that you've aimed for and wanted for yourself as a top-class footballer – all of those ideas are suddenly a reality. In two days' time you're either going to flop or you're going to be a success. Football just works that way – good starts are important. I went through all the crises that you have: am I going to be good enough? Shouldn't I really be playing for a lower-division side?'

Over 21,000 were there to see the former Orient winger's debut. Like all Comfort's debuts it was a memorable one. Middlesbrough ran out 4–2 winners against newly-promoted Wolves, Davenport scoring the third from a pinpoint Comfort cross. The Boro fans instantly took to their exciting new left winger. Comfort says,

'I just had one of those games where every time I got the ball I kept beating people. As a winger that was what I was there to do: beat people and cross the ball. It was almost as if I could do anything I wanted that particular day, and that rarely happens. Maybe it's the adrenalin – you're fired up so much that it's overwhelming.

'As a wide player you're there to do things that people pay to watch, to do something special. If you do, it's amazing how quickly a whole ground can take to you. The reaction was instant. In a football ground, when you get the ball, if there's that expectation you can sense it.'

The manager, Bruce Rioch, flashed a rare smile at the end of the game. He had been under pressure after Boro's relegation and now both his new signings had performed well. Rioch is a ramrod-straight Scot with a commanding presence. As a player with Derby County he was a tough midfielder with an appetite for hard work and a shot like a thunderbolt. His players knew better than to get on

the wrong side of him. Like Alan Comfort, Rioch was
born in Aldershot but his father was in the army. He was
not a tracksuit-and-chewing-gum manager; the smartness
of the parade ground was more his style. According to
Comfort, he ran his clubs on regimental lines too. Players
were expected to do whatever their commanding officer
ordered. Anyone who broke ranks had better beware of
Rioch's unpredictable temper.

'He had the type of personality that could flip from
reacting one way to another very quickly,' says Comfort.
'One particular game, for instance, we were one nil up
in the first half and doing very well. We needed a good
result. Last minute of the half he wants the ball out and
somebody gives it away and we let in a goal. As we came
in everybody was thinking, "What a disaster. We let the
goal in." He just sat down and everything seemed okay.
Then the next minute he picked up a boiling-hot cup of tea
and threw it at one of the players. The mug just smashed
and he went berserk. He said a few things and we thought
he had really flipped. He had that tendency suddenly to
get so overwrought, so angry. And then he would try and
calm himself down.

'Another time (I wasn't in the dressing-room) he got
one of the players up against the wall. Everybody knew
what he was like so you didn't mess around with him.'

Comfort did his best to avoid flying tea cups. He opened
his goal account for Middlesbrough with only his second
game, scoring from thirty yards against Leeds United.
Two games later he was on target again in a 3–3 thriller
against Sheffield United. The early season was a golden
period for the winger. After he had tormented Barnsley
in a 1–1 draw, Rioch commented, 'If we had a striker in
the Martin Peters mould he would get twenty-five goals a
season with the kind of service that Comfort provides.'

Comfort was often tagged as an 'old-fashioned winger',
a throwback to the Stanley Matthews' school of wing play

where you beat players by skill on the ball rather than speed. Looking back on it today, the 1989–90 season was the period when he felt he was fulfilling his promise.

'Here was the place that the whole thing could come together. God had given me the talent to play at that level and I could get it right. Maybe this was as far as I would ever get in football. I believed they (Middlesbrough) would become a first-division team. I wasn't one of the players who thought I could end up playing for England, but I thought that if I could be successful here then I would have got the most out of what I had. For any Christian I think that is essential for you as a person.'

Sadly for Boro, they had no Martin Peters to cash in on Comfort's crosses, and after Gary Pallister's move to Manchester United, the side faltered. By November they were still awaiting their first away win. They went into the north-east derby against Newcastle knowing they needed something to happen quickly if their promotion hopes weren't to vanish with the autumn mist. Comfort was warned by the older hands that until you had played in a north-east derby you hadn't lived. He had already faced Sunderland at Roker Park but high riding Newcastle in front of their fanatical Gallowgate crowd was another matter. It was Alan Comfort's eighteenth league game that season. It was also to be his last.

Like most local derbies, the game was played at a frenetic pace from the start. When the pride of two neighbouring rivals is at stake, the result is seldom an advert for good football. The tension of the occasion and the noise generated by the fans lent a violent edge to the atmosphere. It frequently spilled onto the pitch in a niggling, ill-tempered match with a string of bookings. Ray Ransom, Newcastle's right back that day, was determined that Comfort would feel him breathing down his neck from the kick off.

In the cauldron atmosphere, McGhee cashed in on a

defensive mix-up to give Newcastle the lead in only the third minute. Boro fought back with Proctor equalising from the edge of the box before half time. Then, just after the interval, Slaven sent Comfort through on the left, and when the Newcastle defence failed to clear his low cross, Brennan gave Boro a shock lead.

There was still thirty minutes to go. The game was heading towards a frenetic climax with Newcastle facing an unthinkable home defeat. Players chased every ball to the touchline and tackles were made with bone-shuddering ferocity. The ill-fated moment arrived as Comfort was going for a ball near the touchline with Newcastle's right winger. It was the kind of fifty-fifty ball that players contend routinely in a match.

'We were just trying to get to the ball, one in front of the other, before it went out of play,' says Comfort. 'As we got there we both leant on each other to try and win the ball and as he leant on me, my studs must have got caught in the ground and my knee just twisted. I've seen it on video and you can't imagine it would be as bad as that. But the knee just locked, tucked in, and they couldn't move it. I think they call that shock and damage as well. As soon as it happened somebody summoned up a stretcher straight away and the manager came on and got me off. Everybody knew it was bad but you don't know how bad things are at the time.'

The Newcastle fans booed, thinking Comfort was time wasting, but the catcalls subsided when the stretcher arrived. Comfort was taken to the dressing-room and then rushed to hospital. The club surgeon was at a party that afternoon and had to be telephoned to come to look at the injury. Jill Comfort wasn't at the match that day. She was at home surrounded by packing boxes in the new house the couple had moved into only the previous day. It was Bruce Rioch's wife, Jane, who knocked at the door to break the bad news.

'I was surprised to see her,' remembers Jill. 'I said, "Come on in and if I can find the kettle I'll make you a cup of tea. It's very nice of you to call." She just looked at me as if I was on a different planet. Obviously she thought I would have heard on the radio what had happened and here I was placidly offering cups of tea. She said, "I'm here to get you, Jill. Alan's been injured." I said, "Oh has he? What's happened?"

'She said, "We'd just better get to the hospital." I thought he'd twisted his ankle or pulled his groin. I hadn't been in football long enough to contemplate that injury could actually mean the end.'

No one at the hospital was voicing such fears. Footballers get injured every week. They rest, have treatment and eventually get back in the side. No one expected Comfort to be any different, least of all the player himself. The initial diagnosis was damaged ligaments. The leg was put in plaster and everyone was pleased that surgery wasn't needed. However, several weeks later, the player still couldn't move his leg. The surgeon took another look under anaesthetic but found nothing new. For Alan Comfort it was the prelude to eight months of pure frustration and torment.

'It was a terrible disappointment to be told there was nothing wrong. I couldn't walk, I couldn't move my leg, and they said there was nothing wrong,' he says.

He was sent to Lilleshall, the league's rehabilitation centre, where top sports physiotherapists treated the knee. Comfort remembers it as a period of excruciating pain.

'Because it would never bend they would put elastic things on my knee and they would literally sit on my leg to try and get it to bend – and it wouldn't move.' After a week he was sent back to Middlesbrough with the report that the knee hadn't responded to treatment and needed an operation.

The club surgeon, however, could see no reason why

Comfort wasn't getting better. Time was running out in the season and there were weekly rumours of Comfort's imminent comeback in the press. They were way off the mark – the player was still far from fit. The next solution to be tried was hard training.

'They literally had me, with a leg I couldn't straighten, running round the pitch and up and down hills,' he remembers. 'I'd say, "I can't run. I've got to see somebody." And they'd say, "It's in the mind."'

'I'd argue, "It's not in the mind. I can't go on like this."'

'They'd say, "You've got to keep going through the pain barrier."'

Jill Comfort could tell her husband was in terrible pain and not getting any better. The 'work through the pain' approach was one that infuriated her.

'Inside I would feel very angry. How could they do this? What sort of mentality was it that would say, "Work through the pain"? He was in a lot of pain and he knew that something wasn't right. They were constantly questioning the fact that he wasn't prepared to do it which wasn't the case. How desperately he wanted to get back couldn't be described.'

By this time it was clear that Comfort wasn't going to return for the end of the season. A period of rest was advised. It was at this point that Comfort began to fear that something was seriously wrong with his knee. He decided to take matters in his own hands. One of Jill's uncles was a consultant surgeon in Northern Ireland and arranged for Alan to see Brian Hurson, a Dublin surgeon with an international reputation for treating sports injuries. Within half an hour of examining Comfort, Hurson asked, 'Have you ever thought what you're going to do when you've finished playing football?'

'I've got another ten years before I need to think about that.'

'I think you should start thinking about it now,' was the forthright reply.

The diagnosis was traumatic chondromalacia patellae – in layman's terms a rare disease in the kneecap. Seven months after his injury, it was the first indication that Alan Comfort had that his career might be over. A succession of surgeons confirmed the bleak truth – there was nothing that could be done.

The history of the injury and its treatment can easily be related, but it is almost impossible to describe the mental anguish that Comfort suffered in the months following the accident. Any professional will tell you that being injured is the hardest part of football. To have a long-term injury that shows no sign of improvement, that is thought to be 'all in your mind', that causes you almost constant pain and could threaten your whole career is enough to drive anyone beyond their limits.

The surgeons' verdict was almost a relief in the end. Jill and Alan had prayed that God would be clear about the immediate future: the answer they received was that every surgeon agreed there was nothing to be done. If even one out of three had held out hope, Comfort might have gone on indefinitely trying to get fit and save his career. As it was, he was left in no doubt that he had no future in football. He felt that few people could understand his situation. 'Most people's concept of losing a career is that you're made redundant but you haven't lost your ability to do your job. I had. In my mind I could still play as a twenty-five year old, but physically I was all washed up.

'I had the gift to do something that was very special – people didn't understand that. So they said, "You'll find something else to do." That's true, but it doesn't really deal with it. It is like a bereavement. In the end I think I actually went through a process like losing somebody close to me; the shock of trying to cope.'

There were other losses to come – the nightmare

was only just beginning. From the summer of 1990 the
Comforts started to lose the trappings of a successful
footballer's lifestyle. First the club car had to be returned,
then their brand-new house was put up for sale. They had
watched it being built and moved into it only the day
before Alan's injury. To add to their financial headaches,
Jill had quit her job as a social worker and was expecting
a baby in October. She went into labour in their first
house on an exclusive estate and came out of hospital to
the dismal prospect of a rented house in a downmarket
area of Durham. Until that day Jill feels she coped by
wearing her work hat, actively trying to find solutions
to Alan's injury problem. When she came home from
hospital, her emotional energy had run dry and she went
through a period of post-natal depression. Matters were
not helped by their baby daughter, Sarah.

'She cried virtually non-stop from birth,' remembers
Jill. 'At six months they realised she had a total allergy
to dairy products, so she was a very unhappy little baby
because she was actually in quite a bit of pain. Nobody
realised that – they just thought I was neurotic and
hadn't got her into a routine. But she couldn't sleep, she
couldn't settle at all. We just walked the floors at night.
So it was a hard time. We were just into parenthood,
but Alan was also just into unemployment and trying
to busy himself, to make something for himself during
the days. He had the third bedroom which he tried to
make into a study, but didn't really know what to do
with it.'

Middlesbrough made a financial settlement on their
former player of a one-off payment. There was never a
testimonial for Comfort although some fans campaigned
for it and sparked off a heated row in the press. Although
the sum was equivalent to a year's wages, the Comforts
didn't know when Alan would next earn any income. They
agreed to tie up the money so that it would provide some

interest meanwhile. It meant a dramatic change in lifestyle as Jill explains:

'We were living on benefit but the thing was that we had gone from extremes, not just in finances but in dreams; from being able to have wonderful things if you'd wanted to, to definitely knowing you couldn't have them. If you nearly have a dream, or it is there but only for a fleeting moment, that's much harder than knowing that a dream's not attainable.

'I was going into Sainsbury's with lists that were exact down to pennies, knowing every time that you couldn't go over those pennies, adding it up as you go along, double-checking your adding up by the time you got to the cash desk and knowing that you're going to have to put two items back.

'Another time I remember walking through Marks and Spencers and seeing wool coats with velvet collars for little ones. Alan was with me at the time and my eyes just filled with tears. Tears trickled down my face and Alan said, "What's the matter?"

'"Nothing." It wasn't a big deal, it was just the fact that that was an unattainable dream again. Things that I had as a child but I knew I would never be able to have for Sarah. She was six or eight weeks at the time.'

Three years later, Jill and Alan were having dinner with friends when one of their hosts disappeared upstairs. When they returned they were holding a little girl's coat – wool with a velvet collar. Their daughter had grown out of the coat and they wanted Sarah to have it for the winter. Jill cites it as an illustration of the way she believes that God tailors our lives down to the last detail.

For Alan, the fall-out from his shattered dreams was of a different kind. Once he faced the fact that he wasn't going to play football again, he was faced with a question: what he was to do with his life at the age of twenty-five. The harsh reality of his situation was soon brought home by a trip to the dole office. Faces that had once recognised him with admiration and respect now seemed to stare at him in a different way.

'I didn't want people to feel sorry for me,' he says. 'But to see that look that says, "You got what you deserve. You had it good, now you're like the rest of us," – as a low point that was pretty low.

'I was trying to work out what I would do. Looking through the job sheets, I realised that even the lowest-paid jobs I couldn't do. I couldn't run, couldn't walk, couldn't carry. I'd end up saying, "In fact I can't even do anything."'

With the new football season kicking off in August 1990, Comfort found no shortage of reminders of what he had lost. Ironically one came in the form of a familiar face. Gavin Peacock arrived in Newcastle during November as a £300,000 player with a growing reputation. Living in a hotel hundreds of miles from their families, he and Amanda were only too glad to be able to visit old friends. For his part, he felt deep sympathy for Alan's situation.

'It must have been hard for him, frustrating. I could see that although he felt it was God's will, it wasn't clear what he was doing and where he was going and that was the hard part. He was definitely missing the football. But I didn't feel awkward because Alan didn't make me feel awkward. If you have somebody who's bitter and you can see that they may be jealous, then you would feel awkward. But Alan was just normal and we'd sit there and watch the football on a Sunday if we went round to dinner. They were good friends to us when we went there.'

For all that, Comfort was only human. His career was over at twenty-five while his friend's looked just set to take off. It was inevitable that he battled with a mixture of emotions. He remembers the period as 'a terribly hard time because I was just beginning to see what I'd lost. Gavin arrived and he'd come in and we'd talk about football – and it depressed me no end. I loved talking to him because it was like you were still in it but as soon as he left the house I knew I didn't have anywhere to go. He would be going to training in the morning and I'd be signing on the dole. So in some ways it was really hard having him around because he had everything that I wasn't going to have again. I think I've said to him since that sometimes timing is so wrong.'

The catalogue of footballers whose lives have gone downhill after their careers have ended is probably longer than most clubs would like to admit. As recently as 1993, Tommy Caton, the gifted Manchester City defender whose career was also cut short by injury, committed suicide. Other celebrated cases like Jimmy Greaves have battled with drinking problems. What enabled Alan Comfort to survive his nightmare period was his faith.

At first his reaction to the injury was shock and numbness. During that stage Comfort felt the only way to survive was to hold on to God like a rock in a storm.

'My experience of bad things happening to you in life is that you throw yourself on God all the way. Maybe my life hasn't suffered as much as some other people's, but in my own way, at the crucial moments, I've thrown myself on God. You trust God and you hold so tight that nothing can shake it. I believe that's the way to survive: not to say, "Where's God gone?" initially because you're too weak to do that.'

It wasn't a blind faith that ignored questions, simply a decision to postpone the questions for a later date. When it became clear that his career was over and he was faced with rebuilding his future, then the questions came back. Comfort could think of plenty.

'Was it possible that God had inflicted my injury? It seemed ridiculous. Who did it if it wasn't God? Why did God allow it? If I believed in a God that had control of my life, was I suggesting that God didn't want me to be a football player?

'What was the guarantee of my Christian faith? That I would just survive? I had lost my career, so I was almost at the position of saying that was it. They're frustrating questions because you wonder whether God has lost control and you are just picking up the pieces for the rest of your life.

'When you don't really have an idea of a future, what God is doing becomes so important. I struggled with it but there was no answer to those things. I do not understand why somebody like me, at only twenty-four years old, gets an injury. But for many people, Christians or not, this kind of tragedy is a reality of life. We are left trying to make sense of our own personal circumstances. I don't have all the answers. All I know is that God has my life in his hands and he is trying to work it out for the best. I'm learning to trust that the best will be something that I'll appreciate in the future.'

There were those who told Comfort that God's plan was to heal his knee as a miraculous sign. Comfort believed God was able to do it but simply says that in his situation it didn't happen. Instead what came back into his thoughts was the prediction that Graham Daniels had made several years before that God would call him into the ministry. It was a prospect that half terrified him yet he began to feel sure that this was the way ahead. If he was right, all that he needed to do was convince the Church of England. Had he known, it was a bit like saying that all he needed to do was cross Niagara on a bicycle.

The first hurdle was to talk to Michael Wilcock, the vicar of the church the Comforts attended in Durham. Again Alan went back to his principle of asking God to confirm he was on the right track by giving green lights. If Wilcock had said no then he would have abandoned the idea at the outset.

Fortunately Michael Wilcock gave his backing. Comfort found himself at the beginning of the Church of England's selection process, an obstacle course known as A.C.C.M. On paper he was not the most promising candidate. He was only twenty-five, he had left school at sixteen and never been to college. He had no degree and his main job qualifications were that he could score goals and cross a football with deadly accuracy. If Alan Comfort was to be accepted for the Anglican ministry then he needed a small miracle.

The only thing he had going for him was a burning conviction that God was calling him into the Church. He didn't feel cut out for the job or even certain that he wanted to do it; he only felt God beckoning him. It made the selection process a gruelling ordeal for the former footballer.

'I felt so uncomfortable about a job as a vicar, and yet every time I met somebody I had to try and convince them. Because I'm not from the normal background I had to do more in an interview. I couldn't sit there and say, "I've done a degree in this, a Ph.D. in that. I've worked for a year in this . . ."

'It seemed to me that I had to try and knock them off their seat with the reality of what I was saying. Yet in my own mind I was confused about what had happened to me and also at the back of my mind I was thinking, "I don't want to do this job. Will I really be able to do it?"

Comfort's fears were to do with a vicar's role which he saw mainly in terms of becoming a public speaker. At school he had been one of those children that acquire a dread of being asked to read in front of the class. Following his conversion, he found himself standing on platforms and in pulpits to tell his story as a Christian. Although the reception was usually good, it was never an easy experience as he readily admits.

'I've stood up in front of people with my legs shaking,

forgetting what I was going to say, petrified, believing that if God ever called someone to the ministry it would be the last thing in the world that would happen to me because I haven't the gift to do it. I can speak but I can't sleep the night before. I can't escape the fear.'

All the time he was going through the selection process, the doubts were there. Yet he felt compelled to go ahead. It felt as if God was driving him down a road with no possibility of turning back. Reading the lives of great churchmen as he prepared for his final interview, Comfort found something that struck a chord within him. It was the words of the great Victorian preacher C. H. Spurgeon:

> A man who has within him the inspiration of the Holy Ghost calling him to preach cannot help it – he must preach. As fire within his bones, so will that influence be, until it blazes forth. Friends may check him, foes criticise him, despisers sneer at him, the man is indomitable: he must preach if he has the call of heaven. . . .
>
> He will feel a holy joy akin to that of heaven, and when it is over, he wishes to be at his work again, he longs to be once more preaching.

Alan Comfort copied out the passage and took it with him to read at his selection conference.

'That kind of desire pushes me, and not even football compares with it,' he told them.

Against all the odds, he was accepted to train for the Anglican ministry.

Chapter Eleven

Magpie Mania

In October 1990 Gavin and Amanda Peacock were making a weekend visit to Gavin's family in south-east London. When the time came to return to Bournemouth, they got into the car. 'We've got a two-hour drive back now,' grumbled Gavin.

'Well it could be worse,' replied his dad. 'You could be somewhere like Newcastle.'

Perhaps Jim Smith was listening. Two weeks later he telephoned Gavin Peacock to ask him to sign for the Tyneside club. While at QPR, Smith had let the twenty-year-old midfielder go to Gillingham for a token £40,000 fee. Now, three years on, he was willing to pay seven times that amount to persuade him to play for Newcastle. (The fee was in fact a combination of £150,000 plus Wayne Ferraday in an exchange deal said to be worth £300,000.)

When the phone call came from Smith, Amanda Peacock burst into tears. The move to Bournemouth had seemed like a big step for the London-born newly weds, but they had adjusted and grown to like the beautiful south-coast area where they'd bought their first house. Amanda knew that when Bournemouth were relegated Gavin would

want to move to a higher club – but Newcastle? To her
it seemed like the ends of the earth.

It was a decision they didn't take lightly, but in football
terms Newcastle was a hard club to resist. Every season
has been eagerly awaited by the Geordie faithful as the
one when Newcastle United may awake from its long
slumber and remember its glorious past. It is a club
that once won the league championship three times in
five seasons and has lifted the FA Cup a total of six
times. It is also a city which echoes to the name of
its great goalscoring heroes: Jackie Milburn, Malcolm
MacDonald, Kevin Keegan; even in the hard times there
were Waddle, Beardsley and Gascoigne to watch. The
Geordies are hungry for success, but if they can't win they
at least want their side to play exciting and entertaining
football. As Keegan himself has said, 'What they want,
if you ask them in the town, are two things: they want to
see a great game of football and they'd like to see their
team win. But it's not *"we've got to win"*. That's where
the Geordies differ. We've been clapped off here when I
played, and we'd just lost 4–1 to Fulham. Great game.'

For Gavin Peacock, the trip to Newcastle meant moving
300 miles away from the area where he had grown up. But
there was also a sense of returning to his roots. His father
Keith, a faithful Magpies supporter all his life, says,

'When Gavin went to Newcastle he didn't realise how
deep the feelings were – certainly from my point of view
and my father's – because to play for Newcastle would be
a dream come true.'

Gavin was well aware of his family connections.

'I felt a strange sense of pride putting on a black-and-
white shirt,' he says. 'Although I hadn't thought I'd be
playing for Newcastle, I had those roots up there: my
grandparents are Geordies – they've still got the accent;
my dad's family all come from South Shields. Fifty years
ago my grandad came down looking for work when the

depression was on. He found work in London, stayed and my dad was born down here. It was ironic that I returned fifty years later with my job.

'My first football kit was a Newcastle one. There's a picture of me when I was about seven with my family cousins and me in my Newcastle kit. One of my uncles gave it to one of the local papers and they did a piece on it.'

Having played for QPR, Gillingham and Bournemouth, Peacock knew what it was like to play in three of the league's four divisions. It still gave him little preparation for his arrival at St James's Park. Whereas at Bournemouth his transfer had attracted reports from the local press, at Newcastle there were camera crews and reporters from the nationals waiting to meet him. Fortunately the contract took so long to work out (Peacock wasn't keen to tie himself to the three years Newcastle wanted) that he didn't have to face the press on the first day.

The change from Bournemouth to Newcastle could not have been more dramatic. Where Bournemouth was a quiet holiday resort, Newcastle had all the bustle and noise of a big city. In the Dorset town the football club was only of passing interest to the majority of the population; to Geordies, United is the pride and passion, the banner of their city. Outside McDonalds on Northumberland Street stands the statue of Newcastle's first citizen, Jackie Milburn, right foot in mid air, forever poised to thump the ball into the net. It is a symbol of hope for all Geordies to see.

The stadium stands high and imposing above the town where the cathedral ought to be. During the 1992–3 season, the Lord Mayor of the city kept a fixture list on his desk blotter so that no civic duties could get in the way of the more important business of watching United. Anyone who comes from Newcastle understands such priorities. The Mayor offers Cardinal Basil Hume as an example:

'He was here for a big convention. We had lunch here on the Saturday. As we were going across to City Hall, I says to the Cardinal, "I'm sorry Cardinal Hume. I'm going to miss your speech." He said, "Are you going to the match?" like. I says, "Aye." He says, "Mind if you wanted to do something for me Lord Mayor. . . ." I said, "What's that?" He says, "If they get to Wembley, I want a ticket." '[1]

Gavin Peacock describes his arrival as entering a different world.

'The passion and the fever were such that everyone knew you when you went out. Everybody talked about football all the time. They just live for football up there – it's their whole lives. The social clubs and pubs rely on the football team doing well to take their revenue at the weekend. They say that the atmosphere in them is just dead if we lost, and if we won it was unbelievable. How the team did affected the whole area.'

During the 1993–4 season, 400 pubs and clubs in the north-east were ready to screen Newcastle games on Sunday lunchtimes. According to chairman Sir John Hall, the ground could never be big enough to cater for all the people who wanted to see United's return to the top flight. Beer sales were expected to quadruple in the area.

Amanda Peacock found her husband's instant celebrity puzzling. In hotels and restaurants, waiters would stop to talk about Saturday's game. Strangers would nudge her and ask shyly, 'Is that Gavin Peacock?'

'I suppose it's because of my ignorance of football. I don't realise the importance of it,' she shrugs. 'I was quite shocked at how passionate the fans were there. I was thinking, "It's only a game. Gavin's just doing his job like everyone else." But obviously there are a lot of people who saw Gavin and the others as their idols.'

After spending their first Christmas in hotels, the couple moved to Durham to be closer to friends like Alan and Jill

Comfort and to put some distance between their lives and the football club. But even in that historic city, dominated by the cathedral on the hill, it was soon difficult for Gavin Peacock to walk out on the street without being recognised and accosted. Not that Peacock complains of the drawbacks of fame. He says he has never had an evening out spoiled by fans – they are always polite, sometimes even shy of approaching him.

Magpie mania reached fever pitch in the 1992–3 promotion season under Keegan, but when Peacock first arrived things were not so bright. During the 1988–9 season, Newcastle never rose higher than seventeenth in the (old) first division. They were inevitably relegated, the unlikely import Mirandhina never able to work his Brazilian magic in a team that seemed to change every week. Despite poor results all season, the average home gate was still 22,839 – the sort of crowd teams like QPR and Wimbledon could only dream of.

The following season it seemed that Smith and Newcastle might make a swift return to the first division, but it never materialised. The years of waiting in the wilderness of the former second division had begun.

When Peacock arrived in November 1990, the fans' patience had already begun to wear thin. Gates were down to 15–16,000 which, for Newcastle, was almost the equivalent of a mass walk-out. Peacock was conscious of coming into a side which was feeling the effects of the fans' frustration.

'They were just below half way, something like that. But they'd just missed out on promotion the season before, so everyone was expecting them to be up there again. I was thrown into a pressure situation up there because the crowds were pretty poor by their standard. You could sense in the dressing-room that the players were feeling the pressure. And it was a bit hostile, the fans were getting onto the players a bit. You can hear individual comments if you're near the line, and a general booing if you're doing badly or moves keep breaking down.'

Peacock's debut was eventful. It was a nine-goal thriller at Leicester which ended with Newcastle on the wrong end of a 5–4 scoreline. The following game at Plymouth, Peacock got an elbow in the face in the second half which broke his nose. He stayed on the pitch and scored the winner with an angled left-foot shot. It was a taste of things to come for the Newcastle fans. They instantly took to the newcomer's courageous brand of never-say-die football. He avoided the taunts of the boo boys and the fans voted him 'Player of the Month' in his first spell at the club.

Gavin Peacock ended the season with eleven goals. It was his highest tally yet and the beginning of the period when he would start to attract attention as a goalscorer as well as a talented playmaker.

'If you're looking for spurts or acceleration in a career, mine took off the most in that time,' he says of his three years at Newcastle.

In contrast, Jim Smith's career at Tyneside was only to last until the end of the season. Newcastle missed the promotion boat again and Smith went the way of countless other Newcastle managers who have found it impossible to live in the shadow of the club's great past.

Peacock says he will always be grateful to the manager who gave him his start in football at QPR and then his big break to play for Newcastle. Smith is one of football's great characters – a manager known throughout football as the Bald Eagle. It is rumoured that most of his hair was torn out watching his teams play. Unlike Bruce Rioch whose temper was unpredictable, Smith was consistency itself – he was always a walking volcano.

'He was blood and thunder in the dressing-room, he'd shout and scream,' smiles Peacock. 'You catch some of his facials on the bench – they're unbelievable. I've sat on the bench with him at QPR many times and you'd think that the team were out there playing rubbish and really they weren't. But Jim was so passionate. Then he'd come in after the game and say, "Well done." You'd think, "On the bench he was going mad!"

'Or sometimes he'd come in and throw the odd cup of tea around. Lose his temper a few times with the players. But it was all of the moment, no grudges held. He'd maybe say something to you and then if he felt it was unjust, the next day he'd put his arm round you and say, "Didn't mean that." He was a passionate man who loved football and had genuine feeling for his players. If you went to him with a problem, he'd understand.'

With the notable exception of the Gillingham directors, Peacock rarely criticises anyone he has played for. But his affection for Smith is obviously genuine. On his part, Smith regards his former midfielder as 'a manager's dream', he signed him twice and is on record as saying that given the chance he would make it a hat trick.

The next manager to take over the mantle at Newcastle was as different from Smith as champagne is to red wine. Osvaldo Ardiles signed on April Fool's day but nobody regarded him as a joke appointment. As a player, Ardiles had been one of the most talented and unusual footballers ever to grace the English league. The Argentinian looked a dwarf among giants on the pitch and was so frail he looked as if he might be snapped in two by defenders like Tommy Smith of Liverpool. But with a football at his feet, Ardiles was a magician who could conjure a pass to unlock any defence in the country. In his career with Tottenham he was one of the few foreign players ever to fully win the hearts of English fans. He helped Argentina win the World Cup in 1978 and Tottenham the FA Cup in 1981. The following year he missed the cup final after his countrymen had invaded the Falkland Islands the day before the semi-final. But such was the respect for his

talent and gentlemanly demeanour that he returned to
play football in this country.

Ardiles and Newcastle seemed, on the face of it, an
unlikely combination. But the Gallowgate crowd loved
to see a side that plays good football and welcomed the
Argentinian's promise of a skilful passing game.

As a manager, Peacock found him calm and quietly
spoken but with an immense confidence in himself and
his opinion of the way football should be played.

'Ossie was laid back. If you did something wrong he'd
tell you, but he wouldn't shout or scream or anything like
that. He was very confident in his own ability and in the
principles he had on the game. He could live or die by
them. He liked to play football from the back – attacking
football.'

Ardiles also possessed a mischievous sense of humour
and liked to adopt a relaxed approach in training.

'He'd always be cracking jokes with the lads. He didn't
distance himself in that respect. He'd give you stick and
we would give him a bit back. He'd have us passing the
ball by nicknames only, so you had to shout your mate's
nickname before you passed the ball and it would get
a few jokes going. That was his philosophy – to enjoy
training and enjoy football.'

Peacock's nicknames inevitably revolved around his
religion. 'Father Peacock' or 'The Rev.' were favourites
and, for a short while when he grew a beard, there were
inevitable references to Jesus. Ardiles meanwhile was
always plain 'Ossie'. It is an indication of his relationship
with his team that he was never known as Boss or Gaffer.
Ardiles is a tracksuit manager who likes to work in among
his players rather than six feet above contradiction. He
was ruthless enough to drop players if need be, but also
liked to bring young players through and give them
confidence. During the last six weeks at the end of
the 1990–91 season, Ardiles experimented with a crop

of young players and succeeded in introducing a mellow atmosphere after the tension of the Smith era. According to Peacock, the Newcastle fans responded immediately.

'The crowd liked the way he played football. He totally took the pressure off us. He's so relaxed and confident. He'd just say, "Play. If you make mistakes it doesn't matter, but just keep playing football." The players forgot about the pressure of the crowd and went out and expressed themselves.

'Ossie was good for me individually as a player because I really blossomed under him. He played me in what I regard as my best position – a free role behind the front two in that last six weeks of the season.'

In fact, during the following season Ardiles played a midfield system then unusual in English football: a diamond formation with Peacock roving behind the front two, two players out wide behind him and one sitting in front of the back four. It was a bold innovation and one that suited Peacock who repaid his manager's faith by scoring twenty-one goals. Newcastle's style of play also won them many friends but unfortunately not enough games. Instead of challenging for promotion the side found themselves facing the unthinkable – relegation to the old third division.

Excuses were not hard to find. The side lost experienced players through injury: the prolific Mick Quinn in attack and Bjorn Kristiansen and Ray Ransom in defence. At one point Ardiles was forced to play three eighteen year olds in the back four. His policy of blooding young players was ironically to lead to his downfall. By February 1992 Newcastle were lying periliously in the relegation zone. The directors decided Ardiles' methods had been given long enough to succeed. He was sacked.

Many fans sympathised with the Argentinian and were sorry to see him go. Nevertheless, his departure was a turning point in the club's history. It was to be a transformation in Peacock's career too. He had been relegated with Gillingham and Bournemouth in successive seasons. Now, a year later, he was facing the prospect again. If Newcastle went down then his ambition of playing in the Premiership would be further away than ever.

What happened next is well known. February 1992 will go down in Geordie history as the date Kevin Keegan arrived back at Newcastle. The club were second from bottom of the old second division, £4 million in debt and not a major trophy to show in thirty-five years. Keegan, on the other hand, had won almost every major honour in football. With Liverpool he won three championship medals, three European medals and an FA Cup winners' medal. He was the only British player to be twice voted European footballer of the year. As far as the Tyneside faithful were concerned however, none of this mattered much. The really important fact was that Keegan had finished his career with Newcastle, scoring a goal in his 500th and final league game to clinch the Magpies' promotion to the first division. Keegan was welcomed back as the city's long-awaited messiah.

It was a billing that might have given most first-time managers a few sleepless nights. But Keegan didn't need the job or the money. He had turned his back on a life of comfortable ease in the Costa del Sol to return to Newcastle – and he came back on his own terms. That meant a promise that he would be given the money to build a team that would take the club back to the top flight.

In United's precarious financial position it was a do-or-die gamble, but Keegan had the Midas touch. Within hours of his appointment, ticket sales increased overnight by 10,000 for the home game against Bristol City.

As they came out of the tunnel to a deafening roar, the City players must have felt like they'd been handed a minor walk-on part in a big-budget movie. United were inspired as if the spirit of Keegan was with them on the pitch. The result was a 3–0 victory. Keegan said afterwards that he could have stuck eleven black-and-white shirts on the field with nothing in them and they would have won. A new manager always generates optimism but on this occasion it was more a case of expectation at fever pitch. Peacock played in the game and remembers it as an example of the way a big crowd can almost will their team to victory.

'It was the euphoria. The whole day the crowd carried us through and we played well and we destroyed Bristol City. You could feel the excitement. Keegan didn't do anything in particular, he didn't change anything too much, but he created an atmosphere.'

Sir John Hall, the club chairman, said afterwards that the game put a smile back on the faces of the club's financial backers. But nobody was laughing yet. Newcastle continued to win here and lose there right up to the end of the season. Relegation came down to the very last two games.

The first was against Portsmouth at home. In a tense game, striker David Kelly scored in the last ten minutes to secure a 1–0 win. 'The place just erupted like you've never heard before,' recalls Peacock. 'The relief flooded all over everybody. You could feel it – that relief from the whole of Newcastle that we'd got three points that in effect secured us. But we still went to Leicester knowing that we had to get a result.'

In fact the final game, away to play-off contenders Leicester City, could have seen United relegated if things had gone differently. It was a crunch game for both sides and one where the atmosphere boiled over into ugly scenes at the end. Yet it is one for the scrapbook as far as Gavin Peacock is concerned. He scored the first goal to put the Magpies ahead and set up a climactic finish.

'It was a bad back pass from one of their players. He went to clear it and then decided to pass it back and I was onto it, just clipped it over the goalkeeper as he came out. 1–0 up and then the second half. We hung on and they equalised with about ten minutes to go. 1–1. And we didn't know what we had to do. On the field we were going, "Do we hang on for 1–1? Is that enough?" And they didn't seem to know on the bench. So we didn't know whether we had to go for the win or just hang on for the draw. Then in the last minute of the game our goalkeeper kicked a long ball from a drop kick. I chased it with the centre half in front of me – between me and the goal and the ball. As the goalkeeper came out he poked it past him into the net. I wheeled round to our fans and as I turned round the Leicester fans had invaded the pitch. So I just made an arc and charged off the field. David Kelly had actually gone to our fans and was trapped because the Leicester fans had come straight at our fans. Our fans were trying to pull him over the fence to get him out of the way or else he'd have been battered. He came in. He'd been hit on the head. They'd got a seat or something and chucked it in the air and hit him. We were off at the edge of the pitch. The ref. had blown his whistle as soon as he saw the pitch invasion, but we knew we were safe so we were all celebrating.'

There was a sequel to the climax. Peacock's family come to see him play whenever they can. During his first season at Newcastle, Keith Peacock drove from London to Tyneside and back in one day to see his son play. ('I got taken off,' laughs Gavin.) His parents and Amanda both came to see the crucial Leicester game. They were walking him back to the car when they were faced with a potentially dangerous predicament.

'I was in my Newcastle tracksuit and I thought, "If I see any Leicester fans I'm in trouble,"' recalls Gavin. 'We were walking down this fairly narrow alleyway and we saw this group of lads coming towards us. There was a police van further down and we thought we'd walk faster so that we'd coincide with meeting them around about the police van. As we were getting closer we thought there might be a bit of trouble. And then they started going, "Hey Gavin!" They were all Newcastle fans. One of them took off his tracksuit top and put it over a puddle on the floor. "Don't step in the puddle, Gavin. Walk across there!" They were just delighted.'

It could all have ended differently. A few weeks earlier, after a game against Swindon, Keegan had walked out. Sir John Hall had promised that money would be available but then, having got his man, he was eyeing the size of the club's overdraft. Keegan only wanted the job if he could do it his own way. He got in his Series 7 BMW and drove off. One story goes that he got as far as the New Forest and turned back to sort things out. Another that Sir John chased after him to his Marbella holiday home to make the peace. Whatever the truth, Keegan was persuaded to stay. Players are kept out of such boardroom shenanigans. Peacock says he first heard about Keegan's walk-out through the press. Afterwards the manager told them, 'These things happen. It's nothing to do with you.' And they returned to business as usual on the training ground.

Keegan belongs to a new breed of manager, believes Peacock. 'Ones who are financially independent – Hoddle, Dalglish, Keegan. They don't need the job so they can say, "If the chairman's going to dictate to me, then I don't want it. If I can do it my way then I'll do it. If not, then I won't."'

Keegan soon showed that doing it his way meant expensive changes. He brought in his old Liverpool and Newcastle team-mate Terry McDermott as his assistant and then splashed into the transfer market. He spent liberally but judiciously on players like John Beresford

(£250,000), Barry Venison (£250,000) and Robert Lee (£700,000). When the side looked as if it might flag mid-season he bought Andy Cole from Bristol City for £1.75 million – a player who has not stopped scoring since and one who Keegan believes is a future England striker.

Millions had left the club coffers and everyone knew at the start of the 1992 season that Keegan would make or break the club. Other clubs had spent a fortune and fallen flat on their faces (Derby County did it that season), but Keegan was not a man to wait patiently for success. Geordie fans had waited too long.

'He'd gone for broke, the money he had spent on players,' says Peacock. 'If it didn't work he had a group of highly-paid, expensive players the club couldn't really have afforded. The club has to get 16,000 (gates) to break even on wages and bills, so financially we wouldn't have been able to exist in that first division. Sir John Hall said it himself: "We need to be in the Premiership to function."'

If Keegan's gamble had failed, who knows whether Newcastle would have survived? But from the opening day of the season, it worked. Newcastle set off like Red Rum on valium, winning their first eleven games on the trot and racing into a twelve-point lead by December. It was one of those rare purple patches at a club where a side seems unstoppable. Success breeds success and players just get into the groove of winning. Peacock is aware that he may never experience anything like it again in his career.

'At the beginning it was incredible,' he says. 'It felt like you could take on anyone and win. We felt like world-beaters. If we went a goal down, we felt we could score two. It was a confidence that ran through the team. That's the big thing – the confidence. You see a player who's confident and a player who's not, and they're two different players.'

Peacock has never been a player to lack confidence in himself. What rubbed off on him from Keegan was the determination to win. He says he learnt the secrets of success from the former Liverpool and England superstar.

'You've got to be single minded, you've got to have a resilience when things don't go well and you've got to have a very positive outlook on everything. By the way you think and the way you're confident, you just go for it. He worked hard, Keegan. He works hard as a manager, he worked hard as a player. There's no substitute for that: you've got to put the hard work in. It's a combination of all that. And to sustain the effort for a whole season, to be mentally strong enough to keep that going.'

Interestingly, Keegan himself credits Peacock as one of the most professional and gifted players he's come across. Keegan as a player was a terrier, worrying at the heels of defences and always ready to snap up any half chances around the penalty area. Peacock is similar in his willingness to run at teams until he drops. His father reckons he wouldn't recognise a lost cause if he saw one.

Newcastle sat on top of the first division from 12 September until the end of the season, apart from one seventeen-hour spell where they had no game for two weeks. After Christmas there were a few wobbly moments, but they had given themselves such a cushion it was as if the rest of the division had accepted they were fighting for the scraps.

The season for Gavin Peacock started in triumph and ended with personal disappointment. By any standards he was one of the key players in the promotion push, playing in every game until the end of February when he was sidelined with a hamstring injury. Keegan played him up front alongside David Kelly and before the injury he netted eighteen goals, making him the club's second top goalscorer. Ladbrokes were giving odds at the start of the season against him scoring more than twenty. They must have breathed a sigh of relief when he got injured.

His contribution was much more than goals. In only the second game of the season, club captain Brian Kilcline was injured and Keegan had no hesitation in handing the captain's armband to Gavin Peacock. His immediate response was to play a starring role in the victory over West Ham, scoring one goal and making the second. The captaincy was an honour he kept for most of the season and a tribute to his maturity and leadership when you consider he was chosen ahead of older players like Paul Bracewell.

'There were other players who had been captains at other clubs so you had four or five captains out there,' Peacock points out modestly. 'I tried to lead by example more than talking. By giving 100% and trying to get things going. I'm too out of breath to talk most of the time!'

The hamstring injury robbed him of leading the side into the home straight and the lap of honour. It was hard to miss out on the glory he had done so much to earn. Peacock watched from the stands while new boy Andy Cole scored the goals that secured promotion in his place.

'I don't care what people say, you do feel left out,' he admits. 'Somebody is obviously in the team in your place and if they do well it's going to be hard to get back in. I felt especially frustrated because I'd been captain for practically all the season until I got injured. I'd got eighteen goals and I was looking to get over twenty with ten games to go. Just to finish off the season as captain would have been good.'

Peacock had the consolation of getting back on the substitutes' bench for the last two games of the season. Promotion was clinched in the unglamorous setting of an away game at Grimsby. But the ecstatic Newcastle supporters reserved their true celebrations for the final game of the season at St James's Park. Yet again, poor Leicester City were cast as the victims. It was as if the whole of Tyneside had turned out for a gigantic festival, remembers Gavin Peacock.

'Lindisfarne were playing before the game. There were cheerleaders, people going round in clown outfits. The last people to be considered were the players on that day. We couldn't find much space to do our warm-up. Keegan said to us, "You can go out on a bad note if you're not careful." The opposite happened. We just hammered them.'

Leicester were good enough to have made it to the play offs that year but they were humiliated 7–1. Peacock came on in the second half only to receive a head injury which needed stitches. He returned to warm applause for the last ten minutes of the game.

The trophy was presented after the game and on the Monday displayed to the whole of the city by open-top bus. 300,000 people lined the streets of Newcastle to cheer their heroes. It is a memory Peacock will never forget.

'The amount of people was incredible,' he says. 'You couldn't hear yourselves for the noise. It showed what we had done and what it meant to people. Sometimes you don't think about it because you're playing for yourself, your team-mates and your family and because it's your job. You don't really think what it means to those fans, what a difference it makes to their lives. That really hit home.'

Newcastle had gambled everything on success and won. 'Tell Alex Ferguson we're on our way,' was Keegan's warning to the Premiership champions.

Gavin Peacock meanwhile was on his way back to his London roots and a new challenge. But first he was looking forward to celebrating another promotion – from husband to father. It was to be both the happiest and saddest moment in his life.

Notes

1. Quoted in 'What's Black and White and Scores all over?' by Russell Davies, *Telegraph Magazine*

Chapter Twelve

A Game of Two Halves

During the closing weeks of the 1992–3 football season, when Newcastle were clinching their right to play in the Premiership, Gavin Peacock was rarely seen without a cellphone by his side. There were rumours that some of the big London clubs were about to try and lure him away from the north-east, but the phone wasn't a hotline to his agent; it was in case his wife Amanda went into labour.

The baby kept them waiting until after the season had finished, and when it came there was a shock in store for the new parents. Jake was born without his right hand, the arm ending at the elbow. There had been no warning that anything was wrong before the birth: a freak one-in-a-thousand accident was to blame. Part of the amniotic sac in the womb had wrapped itself around the limb, cutting off the blood supply so that it had been unable to grow.

Up to this point, Gavin Peacock's passage through life appears to have been remarkably smooth. He had grown up in a secure and close-knit family, excelled at school and was fulfilling the promise of an outstanding gift as a footballer. After gambling on leaving QPR at the age of twenty, his rise back to the top of English football had been slow but sure, culminating in Newcastle's promotion to the Premiership at the end of the season. His ambition to play for a top club at the top level was almost within his grasp. The birth of their first son was all the Peacocks needed to make their happiness complete.

Life's hardest blows sometimes arrive when they are least expected. At the moment of the birth, Gavin remembers how his feelings went from one extreme to another.

'You talk about mixed emotions in football and how it can throw you from one high to a low from week to week. The emotions I felt when Jake was born were like nothing I've ever experienced, because it was the happiest I've ever felt in my life and, in a second, when I saw his arm, it was the saddest.

'One of my first thoughts was, "What if there's something else wrong? Mentally or physically. I was thinking as well, being a sportsman, "Will he be able to play sports?" I don't mind if he's not a professional footballer or golfer, I just wouldn't want him to be deprived of a chance to play at school.'

Tests over the next few days showed that Jake was perfectly healthy, and once the first shock had passed, Gavin and Amanda quickly overcame their initial sadness.

'A lot of people have written to us saying they'd had children with similar problems and they'd imagined that we're still in a state of devastation and heartbreak,' says Amanda. 'But we'd really got over that the first few days after he was born because we felt that God had given us Jake for a reason and that he was special. We were really blessed to have him.'

'There are two ways you can go,' agrees Gavin. 'You can either dwell on it and be totally negative – and that's not going to change it. Or you can accept that that's the way he was born and look at the positive side – the fact that there was nothing else wrong. It's amazing that you can be grateful, but it is true.'

Many parents might have been tempted to ask, 'Why did it happen to us?' But the Peacocks never felt those kind of unanswerable questions were relevant.

'We didn't see it like that at all,' says Gavin. 'We felt it was a gift. If anything, a gift from God. All children are anyway. It's the same with Jake. He's got a few inches of his body missing, but it doesn't change him. That's just Jake, that's the way he is. All people have got things different about them. Some have stutters, some people are not accepted at school. Everyone's got their different problems. Jake starts off with a little bit of his problem about his arm, but life's a marathon. You all start off on an equal footing and then we see how it goes. There's a lot of life to be lived for him. I wouldn't put my money against Jake not turning out a better person because of it.'

Although Gavin believes he and Amanda are both naturally positive, he thinks that they wouldn't have come through the situation without their faith. The media did their best to make things harder. With Newcastle's promotion and the speculation surrounding his future, Gavin Peacock was in the spotlight. A Sunday paper in Newcastle pestered them for the story of Jake's birth and, when they were consistently refused, went ahead and made up what they didn't know. Many national papers picked up inaccurate facts from the report claiming that Jake had been tested for brain damage and even suggesting that Peacock needed to get a transfer south to join his wife. As *The Sun* claimed: 'The secret of Gavin Peacock's cut price switch from Newcastle to Chelsea was revealed last night: his newly-born son is disabled. Newcastle dropped his transfer fee by almost £1 million so that Peacock could move back to London to be nearer baby Jake and wife Amanda.'

In fact, Gavin and Amanda were never apart before or after the birth. Peacock also dismisses as 'totally bogus' the idea that the fee of £1.25 million was reduced on compassionate grounds.

The misleading reports were hurtful: friends phoned distressed by the rumour that Jake had been born with brain damage. Peacock dismisses the reports as 'annoying' and prefers to dwell on a more heartening side to the episode. A number of magazines highlighted the way the couple's faith had supported them through the crisis. As a result of the story they received a flood of letters and photographs from other parents whose children were born with similar problems to Jake.

'We've had tremendous encouragement from other people,' says Gavin. 'You do think you're on your own, but the amount of people who have had similar things happen is amazing.'

One effect of Jake's arrival was to confirm the couple's desire to be nearer their families. Keegan had always known that Peacock would eventually return to London and had promised not to stand in his way if the right offer came along. There were rumours that Peacock's old boss Ardiles, the new man at Tottenham, would make a bid, but in the end it was Chelsea's Glenn Hoddle who came in for the midfielder. Hoddle had long been an admirer of Peacock's ability: he had selected him for the first-division representative side and had once tried to buy him for Swindon. At the time, Peacock had preferred to stay in a bid to make history with Newcastle. Hoddle, a Christian himself, had shrugged and said, 'If these things are meant to be, they'll happen.' It was a case of another time, another place. Hoddle accepted the job at Stamford Bridge just at a time when his Republic of Ireland star Andy Townsend wanted to leave and Peacock was looking for a move south. After playing for four clubs in six years, Peacock was prepared to sign a four-year contract and commit himself to London and Chelsea.

He accepts that it is not necessarily a step up from Newcastle. Few will be surprised if the Tynesiders do well under Keegan in the Premiership. Chelsea, in comparison, are older residents among the élite, but have failed to put any silverware in the trophy room since the era of Osgood, Hutchinson and Bonetti. In those days, when footballers sported sideburns to shame the Duke of Wellington, Chelsea was the hub of the swinging sixties and its football stars the fashion accessory to every boutique. When Chelsea beat Leeds in the epic 1970 cup final replay, many saw it as the triumph of flair and style over the 'system' football of Don Revie. Since then Chelsea have remained a fashionable London club but have lived in the shadow of their rivals at Arsenal and Spurs. Hoddle is the sixth manager to take the job at Stamford Bridge since flamboyant chairman Ken Bates took over in 1981. But the former Swindon boss is nothing if not a stylist and Peacock believes he is the man to bring back the glory days to SW6.

'It's a little bit like Newcastle in as much as everybody is hoping that this is the year that something will happen. I think there'll be no better chance than under Glenn: I think he's got the right ingredients as a manager, especially if he's given the money to spend on players. Then I think he'll succeed. It would be nice to be part of it, nice for me to be able to do well at a big club in my home area.'

Ardiles, Keegan, Hoddle – Peacock has now played under three of the greatest names of the previous generation of footballers. It's an experience he believes can only benefit his game.

'Keegan was a bundle of energy and more limited as a player than Hoddle, and yet probably achieved more than Hoddle. Hoddle had all the natural ability and passing. He's good to play with – to learn from the way he plays football. You can learn from just watching him in training.

He's very professional, he likes things done right. He's very organised in preparation for a game: in what you eat, in rest, in set pieces, going over what the other team do as well. Like Ossie, he's got high principles on the game and the way it should be played and he'll stick to that.'

Hoddle had stated his principles before the 1993–4 season kicked off. 'The style of play will be the same as we used at Swindon. It's what I've always believed in: the ball played to feet rather than punted down the channels or over the top.'

It is a style that suits Peacock. He started the season playing up front alongside Tony Cascarino (a player Peacock's dad discovered playing for non-league Crockenhill and took to Gillingham). In the Makita tournament, a curtain raiser to the 1993 season, Chelsea swept aside Spurs at White Hart Lane 4–0 with a Cascarino hat-trick topped by the goal of the game, a twisting header from Gavin Peacock.

'You could see today he's a class act. And I think he's going to get better and better,' enthused Hoddle afterwards of his newest signing.

To repay his manager's confidence Peacock went on to become Chelsea's leading scorer in the opening phase of the season. His goals included the winner against reigning champions Manchester United at Stamford Bridge. When Eric Cantona hit the bar at one end, Chelsea took the ball straight to the other and Peacock arrived at just the right time to hammer home a rebound from United keeper, Peter Schmeichel. Peacock went onto haunt United fans, again scoring the only goal of the game at Old Trafford as Chelsea brought to an end United's 34 match unbeaten run on 5 March 1994.

Whether Hoddle can succeed where others have failed at Chelsea remains to be seen. Chelsea, under the new regime, have started with their familiar habit of flattering to deceive. Much will depend on how long the thirty-five-year-old playmaker can fulfil the dual role of sweeper and manager.

'It's a difficult job to be a player manager in a Premiership side,' acknowledges Peacock. 'You've got to play well yourself and concentrate on your own game, as well as seeing the way the rest of the team are going. If he can do it, he'll have done wonders.'

Hoddle used to perform wonders with casual ease as a player with Tottenham, but bringing back the glory days to Stamford Bridge looks to be the toughest challenge of his career yet.

As for Gavin Peacock, his ambition to climb back to the top flight of English football has been realised; he has already showed that he can more than hold his own among the best in English football. But he still has goals left to achieve.

'I'd like to play at the top level with a top club and Chelsea can be a top club if we're doing well,' he believes. 'I'd also like to play for my country. I figure that I've got the next three or four years where I've got a chance. After that I'll look back and say, "My chance of playing for my country has passed me by." But there's a lot of internationals who probably didn't think they would stand a chance years before.

I suppose it's every schoolboy's dream to play for their country. I never really believed that I'd play for England schoolboys that time when my dad said, "You could be there next year." That made me realise that anything is possible if you put your mind to it. It's a very fine line between being successful and just being ordinary.'

While Gavin Peacock was scoring goals at Stamford Bridge, Alan Comfort was back in the familiar surroundings of Cambridge. Not Cambridge United this time, but at Ridley Hall Theological Training College where he was beginning his final year of training to be an Anglican vicar.

The transition from football star to theology student wasn't an easy one to make. He describes his first year as a 'massive culture shock'. From being used to a certain celebrity as a footballer, he found he was just another first-year student. A typical conversation opener would be 'Where did you do your first degree?' A painful question for Comfort whose only previous college experience had been on day release from football training. Studying was a culture shock for the first year and Comfort found himself yearning to be back on the open spaces of a football field where he could express himself without having to quote learned texts.

Football had finished with him but he hadn't finished with football. When the Bishop of Chelmsford invited him to play in a charity game against Leyton Orient with stars such as Glenn Hoddle and Alvin Martin, he didn't need any persuasion.

At Frank Clark's request, Comfort turned out in the match for Orient and amazingly his knee held up. Two things came of the incident. Bishop Roger Sainsbury, who had swopped his episcopal robes for football kit that day, said to him, 'In three years' time, if you're looking for a job, give me a ring.' It was an offer which was to affect his future later, but at the time Comfort made a mental note and then turned to the *Evening Standard* who wanted to do a story on him. (Several national papers carried 'footballer to vicar' stories that year on Alan Comfort.) Half way through the interview, Comfort mentioned that he was thinking of a comeback in non-league football. A plug would not go amiss. As a result of the story, several offers came in. One was from Ted Pearce, manager of Vauxhall Conference side Farnborough Town and an old friend.

'I've just been coming home on the train and reading this piece in the paper. Would you come and play for us?'

asked Pearce. Comfort was the home-town boy; it would be great publicity for the club.

The comeback lasted until the second game of the season when Comfort stretched for a ball, was tackled and the ligaments went in the kneecap. It was back to the treatment table again for six months. He returned to Lilleshall again and also visited a Cambridge sports clinic in between his studies. He got back in the Farnborough side for an away game against Boston. This time he lasted exactly seven minutes.

That afternoon he lay on a hospital bed, desperately disappointed and ready to give up. It was Ted Pearce who encouraged him to have one more go. He returned for the last six weeks of the season, starting games clinging to the hope that he would just make it to the end. The knee would swell up like a balloon and he was usually unable to walk the next day.

To anyone who isn't passionate about sport, what Alan Comfort put himself through that year sounds like madness. But the desire to play football was in his blood; it couldn't be cut off overnight.

'For that whole year,' he recalls, 'I sat on a physio's table when I should have been studying. Farnborough had their great FA Cup run and I tried desperately to get back. They played against West Ham and I was on the bench. I never played but I was there and involved. Ted Pearce let me sit on the bench because he knew I was desperate to play. That's why he kept saying to me at the end of every injury, "Let's keep going. Let's try."

'At the beginning of the next season he wanted me to play again. I just had to say to him, "I can't go on because it's a waste of time. My knee's never going to be right. I'm never going to be able to play the way I could. Everybody's always going to be disappointed, and me most of all."'

His attempt at a comeback had lasted from July 1991

to July 1992. He admits that with every game he played he thought about returning to professional football. In a pre-season friendly he scored the goal that beat Premiership team Southampton. 'What if you got an offer to come back?' asked reporters. 'I'm doing something else,' smiled Comfort. But inside he knew he would grab the chance with both hands. It never came. In the end he had to admit that he had spent a year chasing a dream.

Looking back today, he reflects that fantasy has always been part of football. 'When you start a game, unless you believe that this might be the one that sends you into stardom, you're wasting your time. Every professional believes that if I play well today, this could be the making of me. We build careers on that. It is all fantasy but it happens – dreams come true in football. That's why I ended up playing for a big club.

'At the end of that year I came to the conclusion that the memories I had were so good and I was destroying them by trying again. There were people I was playing against that I shouldn't have been on the pitch with, yet I was coming down to their level and they were better than me because physically I couldn't cope. It was ruining my own reputation because I'd built something over ten years and I was wasting it.'

Comfort feels it was a year God allowed him to work the football bug out of his system. There were moments when he thought the knee was getting better and he needed to know for certain. At the end he accepted that there could be no more 'What ifs?' It was time to move on and God had clearly shown where he was going.

In his second year of training at Ridley he began to adjust. There were times when he still felt out of his depth but he also began to see that he might have strengths he could draw on. One was the very background that seemed a class barrier in college. The Church, and particularly the Anglican church in modern times, has been justly criticised as a middle-class stronghold in Britain. Alan Comfort feels his roots are different – among people who are more at home in the congregation on the terraces than the one in church on Sunday.

'The one thing I've learned is that God has called me to work with people like me,' believes Comfort. 'I'm not *having* to go. I'm actually saying, "That's me. I can't *wait* to go there." I don't want to go to leafy Surrey, I don't know their problems. I don't understand what it is to have a job in the city and cope with those pressures. In the kind of areas I come from we all read *The Sun* newspaper – and we don't read the front page. Everybody reads from the back in for about four pages then throws it in the bin. Sport is important. Put me in those areas and I know exactly where people are coming from.'

In areas like Newcastle, Sunderland, Middlesbrough, Merseyside and Manchester, to many fans football is god, the sabbath is Saturday and the hymns are the ones you sing on the terraces. In those places people would find it hard to sit through a sermon but they might listen to someone like Alan Comfort.

One person who recognises this is the Bishop of Barking, Roger Sainsbury. He had not forgotten his offer to Comfort after the charity match. The Bishop spoke to Comfort again a year later and their conversation was largely about football. West Ham and Leyton Orient were in the diocese and the Bishop was looking for ways of getting the church involved in those areas. Comfort, who many Orient fans would count among the club's all-time great wingers, was the obvious choice for the job. Part of his brief will be to build bridges between the Church and a football world that can hardly hear its voice.

What does the future hold for Alan Comfort and Gavin Peacock? Life has a habit of bringing us back full circle. St James's Park, Newcastle, will always be a ground which echoes with unforgettable memories for Gavin Peacock.

4 April 1994 was the date he was scheduled to make
his return to Chelsea to play against Newcastle United.
Fifteen years earlier, his father had walked out on the
same pitch to play for Charlton against his boyhood
heroes. This time Gavin Peacock was also going back
as the enemy. Nonetheless, there were many fans in the
Tyneside faithful who had great memories of Peacock
as one of the brightest jewels in Newcastle's glittering
crown.

For Peacock this was the place where it all started. The
ground that launched him as a million-pound Premiership
star. At twenty-five he knows the next few years will
be crucial for him. He has the talent and dedication to
become one of English football's top stars. If Hoddle
can bring back the glory days to Stamford Bridge and
if Peacock continues to attract attention by scoring goals,
his ultimate ambition of playing for England is not out
of the question. With England failing to reach the 1994
World Cup Finals in America, a wholesale change in
the international set-up looks overdue. Players like John
Barnes, Ian Wright and Stuart Pearce know that their
international days are numbered. There is a long queue
of younger players knocking at the door outside. 'All I
will say is that I'm among them,' says Peacock.

Gallowgate is where it all ended for Alan Comfort.
He would trace his first taste of success back to Leyton
Orient in London's East End. In June 1994 he returned
to Brisbane Road in circumstances he would never have
thought possible – as a representative of the Church of
England.

Standing on the terraces at Orient, he could picture
himself exactly five years before – an anxious figure on
the nearside touchline, praying for the referee's whistle to
blow. On that near perfect day he helped Orient to win
promotion in the play-offs and later married the girl of his
dreams in a church 400 miles away. From that high point

his life had seemed to spin out of control from the fateful day at St James's Park which ended his career. He was thrown off the roller-coaster before the ride had ended.

Yet returning to Orient today, Alan Comfort says he felt a strange sense that everything had led up to this point.

'I'm still only twenty-nine years old and my life has been turned upside down,' he reflects. 'But now it offers a new challenge. Looking back on losing my career, there are lots of ways I've changed for the better. I'm less selfish. You were in a career that was just about you: your survival, money, success. Nobody is able to cut across it. It's taken a lot to change that.

'I understand now what it means to have a lot and to lose it. I understand what it is to be helpless for your life, for your own gifts, to lose all of that. I understand what it is to be on an unemployment line and to be humiliated.

'My last nine years have often played host to the tensions of football and God. Both have demanded my total commitment and sometimes I've had to make a choice. I chose God because I knew that in him my life made sense.

'I'm returning no longer as a footballer but I still have a group of people to win over – not with my goals from the left wing, but with my presence in the ground. I don't know what people will make of me but I know one thing – I've returned with a few more answers than when I left.'

Football in some ways is like life compressed into ninety minutes. The struggles, the pain, the moments of frustration, anger, hope and triumph are all played out on a field before us. Maybe that is one reason why sport has had such an enduring appeal. In the end, how you judge a game or how you judge life, all depends on your point of view. Is it all just a matter of luck or, looking back on it, does the result make sense?